Introducing

Jacques Ellul

JACQUES ELLUL

INTRODUCING

JACQUES ELLUL

edited by
JAMES Y. HOLLOWAY

WILLIAM B. EERDMANS PUBLISHING COMPANY
GRAND RAPIDS, MICHIGAN

The essays in this volume first appeared in *Katallagete: Be Reconciled,* Winter/Spring 1970 issue, and are here reprinted with a few corrections, additions, and substitutions by the several authors. *Katallagete* is the journal of the Committee of Southern Churchmen, Nashville, Tennessee 37212. Its editor, James Y. Holloway, and publisher, Will D. Campbell, have been influential in introducing Ellul's thought to readers in the United States.

Acknowledgment is made for permission to quote from the following works by Jacques Ellul: *The Technological Society* (Copyright©1964 by Alfred A. Knopf, Inc.); *Propaganda: The Formation of Men's Attitudes* (Copyright©1965 by Alfred A. Knopf, Inc.); *The Political Illusion* (Copyright©1967 by Alfred A. Knopf, Inc.); *A Critique of the New Commonplaces* (Copyright©1968 by Alfred A. Knopf, Inc.); *The Presence of the Kingdom* (Copyright©1967 by the Seabury Press); *Violence: Reflection from a Christian Perspective* (Copyright©1969 by the Seabury Press); *To Will and To Do* (Copyright ©1969 by United Church Press; A Pilgrim Press book); "Between Chaos and Paralysis" (Copyright©1968 by the Christian Century Foundation).

Acknowledgment is further made for permission to quote from the following: Gary Snyder, *Earth House Hold* (Copyright©1967, New Directions Publishing Corporation); *Malcolm X Speaks* (Copyright©1965 by Merit Publishers and Betty Shabazz); Theodore Roszak, *The Making of a Counter Culture* (Copyright©1969 by Doubleday and Company).

The article "The Revolution: Revisited" by Julius Lester is copyright©1970 by Julius Lester and used with permission of the author and Ronald Hobbs Literary Agency.

FROM JACQUES ELLUL...

I was not brought up in an especially Christian family, and had only a very remote knowledge of Christianity in my childhood. On the other hand, my family was rather poor and I spent all my youth in the midst of the people of the docks at Bordeaux. I began to earn my own living when I was sixteen and continued to do so while completing my university studies. When I was nineteen, I read, by chance, Marx's *Capital*. I was enthusiastic about it. It answered almost all the questions that I had been asking myself. I became "Marxist" and devoted a great deal of my time to a study of his writings. But I was disappointed with the Communists, who seemed to me to be very far from Marx, and I never entered the Party. Around twenty-two years of age, I was also reading the Bible, and it happened that I was converted—with a certain "brutality"!

From that time on, the great problem for me was to know if I could be Marxist and Christian. On the philosophical plane, I realized very quickly that I could not, and so chose decisively for faith in Jesus Christ. But what Marx had brought to me was a certain way of "seeing" the political, economic and social problems—a method of interpretation, a sociology. So it did not seem impossible to utilize this, starting with the Christian faith. I could not accept the view that there should be a Christian faith without social and political consequences. On the other hand, however, I saw clearly that one could not deduce directly from the Biblical texts political or social consequences valid for our epoch. It seemed to me that the method of Karl Marx (but not of the Communists!) was superior to all that I had encountered elsewhere.

5

In 1933, I participated in the founding of the journal, *Esprit*, with E. Mounier, thinking that in this group we would succeed in doing what I saw somewhat vaguely. After several years, however, I realized that they were heading towards ordinary socialism. I also clashed with the very uncompromising Catholicism of Mounier. I then took my road all alone, for in my contacts with Social Christianity, I realized that it was not serious theologically, and was very superficial from the viewpoint of sociological analysis.

Since 1935, I have been convinced that on the sociological plane, technique was by far the most important phenomenon, and that it was necessary to start from there to understand everything else. My first article on technique dates from 1935. Since that time, I have given myself to the task, on the one hand to deepen my theological and biblical knowledge and, on the other hand, to continue with a sociological analysis of the Western world. I have sought to confront theological and biblical knowledge and sociological analysis without trying to come to any artificial or philosophical synthesis; instead, I try to place the two face to face, in order to shed some light on what is real socially and real spiritually. That is why I can say that the reply to each of my sociological analyses is found implicitly in a corresponding theological book, and inversely, my theology is fed on socio-political experience. But I refuse to construct a *system* of thought, or to offer up some Christian or prefabricated socio-political solutions. I want only to provide Christians with the means of thinking out *for themselves* the meaning of their involvement in the modern world.

Such is the essential goal of my work. It ends, necessarily, in a Christian ethics—but *only* therefore an ethics that is indicative.

JACQUES ELLUL is Professor of the History and Sociology of Institutions in the Faculty of Law and Economic Sciences of the University of Bordeaux and at the Institute of Political Studies. He was born in Bordeaux in 1912, is married and the father of three children, and holds degrees in history, sociology and law and an honorary doctorate from the University of Amsterdam. In 1937 he was appointed director of studies at the University of Strasbourg, was dismissed by the Vichy government in 1940 and reinstated as Professor of Law at the University of Bordeaux in 1944. From 1936 to 1939 he was active in French politics, and from 1940 through 1944 a leader in the French Resistance. He was deputy mayor of Bordeaux from 1944 to 1946. He abandoned his political career in 1947. M. Ellul was a member of the Committee on Work of the World Council of Churches from 1946 to 1953. He is a member of the National Synod and of the National Council of the Reformed Church of France, and director of the journal *Foi et Vie*. He has written twenty-one books — six on the history of institutions, seven in sociology, and eight on theological or biblical themes. He is also the author of more than a hundred articles.

THE FOLLOWING BOOKS BY JACQUES ELLUL
ARE AVAILABLE IN ENGLISH:

The Theological Foundation of Law (Doubleday, 1960; Seabury, 1969)
The Technological Society (Knopf, 1964)
Propaganda (Knopf, 1966)
The Political Illusion (Knopf, 1967)
A Critique of the New Commonplaces (Knopf, 1968)
The Presence of the Kingdom (Seabury, 1967)
Violence: Reflections from a Christian Perspective (Seabury, 1969)
To Will and To Do. Part I of Volume One: Introduction to a Christian Ethics (United Church Press, 1969)
The Meaning of the City (Eerdmans, 1970)
Prayer and Modern Man (Seabury, 1970)

CONTENTS

INTRODUCTION

For a number of years the writings of Jacques Ellul have been important to the Committee of Southern Churchmen. Their importance has been reflected often in the pages of our journal *Katallagete: Be Reconciled*. This interest and concern culminated in the publication of a special double issue of *Katallagete* devoted entirely to essays interpreting and responding to Ellul's ideas, especially his social analyses. The present volume reprints those essays, in order — as the title suggests — to introduce concerned people to the insights of Ellul.

The Committee of Southern Churchmen believes that Ellul's exposition of the Bible is an authentic expression of the Christian faith. Introducing the first of several volumes of his Christian Ethics, Ellul wrote:

> I . . . confess that in this study and this research the criterion of my thought is the biblical revelation, the content of my thought is the biblical revelation, the point of departure is supplied by the biblical revelation, the method is the dialectic in accordance with which the biblical revelation is given to us. . . . (*To Will and To Do*, p. 1)

We are convinced that such exposition is essential to the Christian life: in the first issue of *Katallagete* we noted an agreement with Karl Barth, being "prejudiced in supposing the Bible to be a good book" and "profitable for men to take its conceptions at least as seriously as they take their own." Moreover, we still have little interest in the Christian social action and the Christian-in-politics—liberal or conservative. We maintain our misgivings about Christians and their ecclesiastical bureaucracies who can find no way to express their commitment to Christ but in the prevailing political radicalisms, right

11

or left. We believe that the only task put upon the Christian as Christian is the life (the *being*) of reconciliation described by St. Paul in II Corinthians 5:15-20. If it be argued that we have no "strategy" or "plan of action" to offer in the place of the ones we reject, we plead guilty. We stand as Christians without strategy or plans. We see no witness in following the idols of modernity or travelling roads-to-nowhere simply to carry out "plans," as if that were "getting things done." For the Christian to succumb to the world's definition of "action" is to tell a lie about what God has "acted" in Christ. Most of these convictions (or "prejudices") are eloquently and effectively expressed by Ellul's theological writings.

We are similarly attracted to Ellul's social analyses. Since completing patriotic chores in the mid-'forties we have known in our bones that something is fundamentally wrong with society—ours, the Soviet Union's, China's, Britain's, Egypt's, Israel's, etc., etc. . . Ellul's description of the technological society speaks clearly and we believe accurately about what is going on and about where we are heading. It is not a question of misguided leaders or conspiracies of bad people; if it were, the frantic efforts of the politicians and political revolutionaries—right and left, each with their own Christian enthusiasts—would have produced at least *one* sign of hope in the past thirty years. But the question *does* seem to be in large measure the technological determinants (not yet, perhaps, inevitabilities?) that are at the center of Ellul's social analyses.

In a word, Ellul speaks to our guts and our heads.

But we can be more specific than that. We are not referring primarily to the disorders, crises and adjustments that have made up the agenda of the social scientists and the churches' specialists on social action for the past thirty years—although we are talking about that, in part. We are talking primarily about the issues that hit *our* guts, about what has happened and is happening to us and to those closest to and around us. We

12

suspect these same issues hit many others, also in the gut. That is the *why* of this collection of essays. We are talking about the gut as well as the head issues that Ellul speaks to *us* about — that is, *not* to "our" churches, denominations, political parties, schools, neighborhoods, clubs, etc., etc., because these seem increasingly abstract, less and less real, less and less where we are today.

We are talking about finishing high school, possessing advanced degrees from all sorts of pompous and Ivy League universities—and seeing that we are now less knowledgeable, less wise, less free with all of our knowledge than parents who did not finish grade school and grandparents who could read only the numbers on a carpenter's rule and price-labels at the county store. We are talking about our labor in "education," knowing that what we do is less credible than what we received when "given an education" twenty or thirty years ago.

We are talking about ourselves and brothers, cousins and friends who knew the threat which haunted fathers and uncles and neighbors about being "laid off" during the depression of the thirties—and see ourselves, brothers, cousins and neighbors now, economically as secure as any class of people in history, but at the same time and because of this security, less free spiritually, less real as human beings with each other and with ourselves, more beholden (read "enslaved") to the powers of mill or company or school or church or business or bank or building and loan company for whatever "freedom" and "meaning" we can wrench from these damnations of our lives. We see life and value defined by the mill and the company, not by God—or even by ourselves. We see in the midst of our affluence and security almost no joy or kindness, but instead an aura of ruthlessness and inhumanity that pollutes every human relationship from sex to war.

We are talking about the fact that we went through the depressions of the thirties and look at our children and our brothers' and cousins' and neighbors' children

13

now--financially independent beyond what most of us could have defined thirty years ago, able to afford every necessity/luxury (indistinguishable in the technological era). But our children are less free than we were two decades ago (and we less than our parents and grandparents) and become less free with each ticking of the clock as they (and we) become more materially secure by our beholdenness to the state and its networks which surround everything that any of us do. We see them (and us) beset by more terrors and threats than we (or any middle-aged psychiatrist) could possibly imagine. We see that they have known life only under the threat of atomic-hydrogen-germicidal-ecological apocalypse. Less free, less alive because less human, we see their expressions of contempt for the culture which identifies us the parents, and/or their hatred and violence at the black and the poor who will not or cannot assimilate into this culture of the damned.

We are talking about marching off to war twenty or thirty years ago with misgivings but without protest and returning home, warned by society and church that we must devote effort and intelligence to keeping abreast, indeed, participating in "Politics!". ("An enlightened electorate is the foundation of democracy.") But this very passion to be political and to-keep-abreast is now one of the principal ingredients of the totalitarianism of contemporary society, and the "social action" of the Church has done a great deal to forge this totalitarianism. We see the young men who with us were part of democracy's fight to "unconditional surrender" in 1945 as the leaders of two decades of life under God which spends more than a trillion dollars on war (including especially "space" exploration), yet helpless in the face of the unparalleled human sufferings of political messianisms, racism, hunger, disease, the piling of people on people in urban centers and "underdeveloped" nations, creating thereby technological crises that *are insoluble*, despite

14

official cant, piety, or good intentions that they can be solved.

We are talking about the hope poured into us when we went to school with the G. I. Bill and heard the analyses and the promises of the academicians (especially the social scientists) about the great problems that were the great *challenges!* to our youth. But what they then called "An American Dilemma" has always been "an American *tragedy*": All signs everywhere showing that we are satisfied to face the challenges of racism, war, technological totalitarianism, and environmental poisoning by what is at this moment the faith of the liberal-totalitarianism of white, affluent Americans, using the environment and tools of the contemporary technological garrison state. We are talking about the churches' sponsorship of these very developments by their current preoccupation with "future" and "hope" defined not by Jesus Christ but by technology and a hodge-podge of secular ideologies.

We are talking about being warned from childhood to move into the convenience of the city (or at least into a town with five thousand or more inhabitants), away from the impoverishment, ignorance, inconvenience and general backwardness of the "country." Now we find the hell-holes of the secular city, controlled in police-state fashion by a frightened and therefore arrogant, reckless and totalitarian white middle class, and celebrated by a wide variety of Christian theologians and in the bureaucracy and theology of our churches.

We are talking about the best, most enlightened and liberal segments of American society—labor unions, anti-prejudice leagues, foundations, liberal political groupings, colleges, universities, church groupings—becoming agencies which use and are used by agencies of the state to *get* "the other side"—Vietnamese, hippies, Kluxers, Bolivians, Weathermen, Panthers, etc., etc., etc.

These are the matters of the guts to which Ellul's

writings speak. We believe, as he does, that these matters are fundamentally theological—which is to say, they are issues about which the Christian faith pits its word and its life. We believe that the efforts of church and society to understand these issues by data-into-computer, by relevance-in-a-world-come-of-age or by theological "scholarship" is dishonest or hopelessly misdirected. We believe that Ellul's account of the meaning of the technological society is the most accurate framework within which we can understand what is happening to us. We believe, with Ellul, that ecclesiastical as well as political "reform" as currently practiced is today futile. Such reforms are inevitably marginal; they deal with matters of forms and images on the periphery of things. They are a misleading and therefore dangerous rearranging of the furniture which will eventually be absorbed by and thus reinforce the technological garrisonism of contemporary state and society. We believe that Ellul's judgments about the tasks before the Christian in this society are theologically and ethically accurate and therefore matters of Either/Or for the Christian. They offer — to those who will see them as such — the options we have sought to put before the readers of *Katallagete* for five years.

We believe these options are the real and viable ones. Thus we cannot accept the charge that we have merely cursed the darkness instead of "lighting a candle" of a political involvement here, a protest march there, a signed petition elsewhere, a maneuver for church reform yonder, a court suit day before yesterday, an appearance before Congressional committees tomorrow. These things will be done quite apart from what *any* Christian does about them: what, then, does the Christian "witness" or even contribute, in these affairs? Moreover, there is always Matthew 5:46-47. The problem of Christians-for-McCarthy, Kennedy, McGovern or Weatherman is the perversion of their determination to be a *Christian* "witness" by the Baalism of modern politics. Thus Larry O'Brien, Richard Goodwin and Tom Hayden are freer

16

and more effective than the Christian-in-politics-as-Christian. The Christian should be free, not to throw stones but to draw attention to the illusory quality of modern political efforts. What has political "reform" accomplished in the past thirty years? Likewise church's "reform." What is the point of Christian-as-Christian "lighting a candle" in politics, church business, protests, etc., etc., when it illuminates not the "darkness" but instead serves as a beacon celebrating the Baalisms, the perverseness of modern society?

Nor do we accept the charge that we are merely preaching Stoic *Schadenfreude* in the guise of Biblical fundamentalism—expressing a wholesome joy at the surreptitious totalitarianism that rises sight unseen upon the ruins of a disintegrating society. Our pessimism, with Ellul, is with man, not God. To underline our answer to this charge, we quote our agreement with Ellul's judgment: ". . . in the present social situation, there is not even a beginning of a solution, no breach in the system of technical necessity." The best ideas, solutions and actions are assimilated for its own use "into the technical framework which renders them spiritually worthless." The technical determinants are not yet inevitabilities. But "if man—if each one of us—abdicates his responsibilities with regard to values; if each of us limits himself to leading a trivial existence in a technological civilization, with greater adaptation and increasing success as his sole objectives; if we do not even consider the possibility of making a stand against these determinants, then everything *will* happen as I have described it, and the determinants *will* be transformed into inevitabilities." (*The Technological Society*, p. xxxi, p. 424, p. xxix)

That is the option. . . .

— JAMES Y. HOLLOWAY, Editor,
— WILL D. CAMPBELL, Publisher,
for the Committee of Southern Churchmen

WEST OF EDEN

JAMES Y. HOLLOWAY

The environment that now encloses the activities of individuals and communities is *essentially* different from the environment of a hundred, perhaps even fifty years ago. This judgment on the significance of the technological era is not unique with Jacques Ellul, but his writings as sociologist and theologian are characterized by a single-minded devotion to the task of exploring the meaning and the consequences of this essentially new environment. Technique, Ellul believes, has delivered man into this new environment. Technique may or may not determine man more than nature determined him in the past, but the critical fact is that man is determined *differently* by the environment of technique in the present era. This technical determinism—especially the determinism resulting from the conjunction of technique and the state, which Ellul regards as the "most important phenomenon in history"—this technical determinism accounts in large measure for the frightening and yet increasingly uniform political and social activity by every ideological expression and every value-system in every corner of the world. Similarly, this new environment of technique has altered the direction, *but not the nature*, of the witness of Christians and Christian communities.

Hence the title of this essay: "*West* of Eden": the contrast between the environment of nature-and-history—

JAMES Y. HOLLOWAY is editor of *Katallagete* and teaches political philosophy and Christian ethics at Berea College, Kentucky. With Will D. Campbell, he is the author of *Up To Our Steeples In Politics* (1970).

"*East* of Eden" into which God cast man following the sin in Eden—and the contemporary, artificial, non-historical, un-natural environment of technique—"*West* of Eden," the world in which technique became the power enclosing and dominating man as he pursued industry, science, technology, political messiahs.

Ellul has frequently reminded Christians of their responsibility *as Christians* to come to a realistic understanding of the socio-political world in which all men live. This is necessary, he believes, not only to understand the direction of the witness by the Christian in the world, but also to make certain that that witness is distinctively Christian and not unwittingly efforts in support of a moribund ideology of political and social systems that merely intone the name of Jesus Christ at selected intervals. Ellul's own work seeks to carry out just this responsibility. His sociological and political analyses are written under the demands he knows as a Christian, and it is precisely because of this commitment that he judges it dishonest as well as meaningless to introduce "Christianity" as an authority for these writings. Instead, his sociological and political analyses are a pole for his theological and biblical writings—"compositions in counterpoint," he calls them. These "compositions in counterpoint" are in no sense a Tillichian "theology of *correlation*." Rather, Ellul is composing a "theology of *confrontation*"—the Biblical message written to confront the developments (especially the technical developments) in modern society. His work, he explains, has from the first turned on "the contradiction between the evolution of the modern world [notably the technical evolution] and the biblical content of revelation."

The keystone of these efforts to grasp the meaning of the modern world is his *The Technological Society*. It is important to direct attention to the environment he describes there, inasmuch as it provides the context for his other sociological and political analyses. Moreover, the recently published *The Meaning of the City* is, by his own account, the theological study that corresponds to this analysis of technique, so there is now available in English for the first time one specific expression of his "compositions in counterpoint": sociological analysis—theological analysis.

It will be necessary, therefore, to summarize Ellul's definition of technique and so explain how the character of modern technique has, in the past century or so, radically, decisively, and irreversibly permeated and then determined political, social, scientific, and economic activity.

What immediately follows is little more than a paraphrase of segments of Ellul's *The Technological Society*. Today, Ellul explains, technique *"is the totality of methods rationally arrived at and having absolute efficiency* in every *field* of human activity." (p. xxv, italics his) Technique does not mean and is not reducible to machines, technology, or this or that means or method for attaining an end. Machines, technology, methods for attaining ends are included within technique; technique drives them, but it is not identical with any one of them. Ellul insists that his definition—"the totality of methods rationally arrived at and having absolute efficiency in every field of human activity"—is not a "theoretical construct." Rather, it was "arrived at by examining each activity and observing the facts of what modern man calls technique in general, as well as by investigating the different areas in which specialists declare they have a technique." (p. xxv)

Yet the critical factor in Ellul's analysis of technique is not the definition, or technique's "intrinsic characteristics." Rather, it is the *relationship* between technique and society. This relationship accounts for our society being properly defined as "the technological society," and explains why the character of technique, in earlier societies, is fundamentally different from its character in our society. Early sections of *The Technological Society* are devoted, in some detail, to the distinction between traditional techniques and modern techniques. "Today's technical phenomenon has almost nothing in common with the technological phenomenon of the past," he explains. Indeed, the characteristics of the *relationship* of technique, society and the individual—the critical factor for Ellul's analysis—up to the eighteenth century have all but disappeared. In previous societies, technique was applied in certain narrow, limited areas, geographical as well as technical—techniques of production, war, hunting, etc. This permitted a technical diversity between localities, and also reserved the possibility of some human choice in the technical process. Moreover, human progress was not tied up with technical progress. But "in our civilization, technique is in no way limited."

> It has been extended to all spheres and encompassed every activity, including human activities. It has led to a multiplication of means without limit. It has perfected indefinitely the instruments available to man, and put at his disposal an almost limitless variety of intermediaries and auxiliaries. Technique has been extended geographically so that it covers the whole earth. It is evolving with a rapidity disconcerting not only to the man in the street but to the technician himself. It poses problems which recur endlessly and ever more acutely in human groups. Moreover, technique has become objective and is transmitted like a physical thing; it leads thereby to a certain unity of civilization, regardless of the environment or the country in which it operates. We are faced with the exact opposite of the traits previously in force. (p. 78)

The penetration of technique has been so massive that Ellul insists that the primary environment of man in advanced societies is no longer nature, but technique. Our problems are less and less "natural" ones (floods, earthquakes, geographical distances, etc., etc.) but "technical" ones (air and water pollution, atomic and chemical "fallouts", noise, the inhumanity of the state, indeed, all bureaucracies, administrations, etc., etc.). We are aware of this when an overt one calls it to our attention—filth and waste are dumped into a water supply, broken oil lines or the hulls of tankers killing fish and birds and spoiling the middle-class vacation beaches; or, garbage pile-ups, airline and automobile tie-ups and crashes, ice-storms downing power and communication lines, television news and commercials, stripmining, education, Medicare inequities and exploitations, Social Security injustices, the dismissal of a bureaucrat who discovers waste and mismanagement in his own agency, urban smog, wiretapping, Vietnam, "Mission: Impossible"—these are not the problems between man and nature or even man and history, but man and technique.

Ellul's case turns on his conviction that technique is not one factor which can be isolated from other factors in society. Rather, technique *encloses* political, social, scientific and economic activity in such a way that politics, science, economics, social activity, etc., do not determine and direct technique. *The political, social, scientific and economic world today is defined by its relation to the world of technique.* In a word, what determines our politics, our economics, our science, our social activities is technique. Politicians, economists, scientists? . . . *no human choices* determine or direct technique.

It is possible here merely to summarize very briefly Ellul's discussion of the characteristics of technique which have fashioned what he calls "the technological society." Again, it is important to remember that what is paramount for Ellul's analysis is not "the intrinsic characteristics of technique" but "*the characteristics of the relation between the technical phenomenon and society.*" (p. 63, italics added) What follows is an effort to direct attention to this relationship which has resulted in "the technological society"—that omnivorous world which obeys its own laws, no longer rests on tradition, is no longer determined by the choices or the values of men, but rather obeys its own previous technical procedures. Ours is the era, as Ellul has emphasized in all of his works, where goals have become identical with the perfections of *means*, methods. . . . The means *is* the end: that is the meaning of the technological era.

There are, he explains, two distinguishing characteristics of *modern* (not ancient) technique which are the foundation of its other characteristics: these are "rationality" and "artificiality." Taken together, "rationality" and "artificiality" suggest the criteria of technique: *efficiency*. By "rationality", Ellul means that anywhere technique is applied, a process is present which tends to bring mechanics to bear on all that is spontaneous or irrational—e.g., any system, division of labor, standardizations, norms of production. Examples are obvious: *registrations* for any human action: for the draft, as a "resident alien," for college and for college courses, for income and other tax efforts of modern government, for social security, for unemployment compensation or for employment in any large industrial concern, business corporation, government service. Perhaps the most obvious example of rationalization to many of us is the proliferation of *administration* in education, church, science, government, business, industry, etc., in the past forty years, so much so that administration is now *an* end in itself, and bids fair to become *the* end of all endeavors in post-industrial, technological societies. This is reflected in the battles, East and West, between students and "administrators" (the faculty, impaled on their "objectivity," resolutely plagues both houses) about higher education in today's world. Or, the increasing dependence of the Church ("Crusades for Christ," "Look Up and Live," Oral Roberts, etc., etc.) on technique to proclaim the Gospel: it matters not *what* is said, so long as the *means*, the *methods* . . . are effective! Administration is concerned less and less with ordering and counting paperclips, but more and more with the efficient *means* of counting the paperclips—thus, computers, comptrollers, programmers, etc., etc. Administration, in other words, is today chiefly and by definition concerned with the administration of administration. The question

24

is not whether all this is "bad." It *is* a question of the inevitability of it, if men and institutions are to "survive" in the technological society.

Moreover, this rationality affects human nature and human activity. One thinks of the increasing rationalism of the "state"—chiefly defined now by its bureaucrats and technicians, not merely in the Labor Department, the welfare offices, the Defense Department, but in the State Department and White House. One also thinks of the bureaucrats and technicians who make up so much of the administration and the teaching end of education— in the departments of political science, sociology, economics, philosophy, "religion," etc., etc. Most obviously, what is called "education" in the United States has become little more than *technique*—methods, materials, means. The following words of the concerns of the American Association of Collegiate Registrars and Admissions Officers make the point:

> In academic transcript relationships a due regard for fair play to students and to institutions concerned suggests the reconciliation of any conflicts in responsibilities according to the following priority: A regard for a transcript as a complete educational record without omissions. . . . A college or university transcript is a copy of the complete unabridged educational record of an officially enrolled student issued for the purpose of communicating information about the student to another institution, agency or individual.

All as if the most monumental fiction in education were not the students' . . . *transcript!*

Indeed, when "education" is other than technique, it is not the concern of "education," and is usually attacked with ruthlessness by professional educators. "Education" today concerns the *how,* to arouse, to stimulate, to motivate, to adjust, to assimilate the pupil, with little regard to the substance or the content of the arousal. Thus, a successful "educator" becomes an educational bureaucrat/ administrator. The "artificiality" of the educational bureaucracy has inflicted itself on all classrooms in ways that may spell the end of the peculiarly American messianic dream: salvation through education. The writings of Jonathan Kozol, John Holt and George Dennison document one part of this tragic story. Another is the plight of the social "sciences" (and, slowly but surely, the soft disciplines, beginning with "history" and ending with philosophy, religion, aesthetics), which transmit information and series of statistics recording the pseudo-events (the major "news events") of the technological era. That is why there is substance to the charge made by students in universities the world over that "education" equals brainwashing-by-the-establishment.

> . . . the highest virtue demanded of man today is adjustment. The worst judgment a man can suffer is to be called maladjusted. (Maladjusted to what? Very exactly, to the technological society. Sociologists and psychologists are agreed in acknowledging that technology is the most frequent cause of maladjustment.) The chief purpose of instruction and education today is to bring along a younger generation which is *adjusted* to this society. (*To Will and To Do*, p. 192. Ellul's italics)

And that is why so many leaders in the Black communities and those in the forefront of arts, letters and music in the United States are *not* products of "the American system of education." (One notes, significantly, that Herbert Marcuse does not include "freedom *from* contemporary education" in his lists of urgent "freedom *froms*" in post-industrial societies.)

Finally, the "rationality" of technique explains the hiatus between the reports of governmental bureaucracies and the actual performance of these bureaucracies—for example, in meeting poverty in the United States. Paul Good's "Poverty in the South" (*The New South*, Winter 1968 and later, his *The American Serfs*) calls attention to this hiatus throughout his study. The reports of the Kerner or Walker or Eisenhower Commission are vivid documentations of why bureaucracy—by definition "rational"—cannot meet the stubborn fact of the existence of violence and starving human beings in an affluent, over-fed society. What is involved is more than the intransigence of a Senator Eastland or a Senator Ellender or the hawkishness of Dean Rusk or L. Mendel Rivers. If it were simply senatorial viciousness, why has the poverty of East Harlem *not* been eliminated? Why would Bedford-Stuyvesants be allowed to develop in parallel to Westchesters in New York state —the state which most closely approximates Mississippi in the number of poor people obtaining food from the United States government: the state of Senators Javits and Goodell, and Kennedy, Lehman, Wagner, etc.? Ellul's exposition of this "rationality" in political life goes a long way to explain Murray Kempton's observation that as America's crises grow worse, our "Reports" on them (Kerner on "civil disorders," Eisenhower on "violence") get better.

The other chief characteristic, "artificiality," refers to the fact that technique opposes nature. Technique is obviously not natural, but artificial, a man-devised artifact of means and methods. The technique of means and methods functions artificially, the effect of which is to subordinate, or eliminate, the world of nature. Obvious examples are hydroelectric dams (waterfalls are absorbed into them), and stripmining (coal used for generators). Technique cannot permit the world of nature to enter into even a symbiotic relation with it. (Ellul seems to suggest that *technique*, which has made stripmining not only possible, but has created the problem of the consequent devastation of nature—technique cannot be invoked "to solve" the excesses of stripmining by "reclaiming" the nature it has destroyed. At best, "reclamation projects" will create technical problems other than the initial ones—created by stripmining—but technique cannot enter into a symbiotic relationship with nature. The problems of air pollution—and their technical solutions—suggest the parallel. The polluted air all

27

but eliminated the bird population in London, England, for decades. With the techniques required by law to reduce air pollution, the birds have returned—in hordes and with a vengeance—but not in a symbiotic relationship with the techniques that made it possible for them to return.)

There are several corollary characteristics of technique as Ellul has described it, characteristics which increase in importance as technical civilization progresses. The most important of these are technical automatism, self-augmentation, monism, universalism, and autonomy. Each must be explained briefly. (On what follows, see *The Technological Society*, pp. 79 ff.)

Automatism of technical choice simply means that when all calculations are in, and the most efficient method decided upon, *the technical movement becomes self-directing*. Newspapers talk about this every day when they report the newest devices for strategic warfare in Vietnam and elsewhere. Napalm and the Lazy-dog and the Side-winder missile—even the A-bomb—are products of automatism. At a certain stage in the technical development, the technical movement becomes self-directing: The thing then *has* to be used. In 1954, Ellul wrote: "A surgical operation which was formerly not feasible, but can now be performed is not an object of choice. It simply is. . . . Technique itself, *ipso facto* and without indulgence or possible discussion, selects among the means to be employed. The human being is no longer in any sense the agent of choice. . . ." It is wrong to say that man is the agent of technical progress, or that he can choose among possible techniques. Man is merely a device for recording effects and results obtained by various techniques. He does not make a choice of complex human motives. "He can decide only in favor of the technique that gives the maximum efficiency. But this is not choice, for a machine could effect the same operation." (p. 80) So Ellul in 1954. Fourteen years later, John Lear, science editor of the *Saturday Review,* wrote in the issue of March 2, 1968: "The recent epidemic of human heart transplants (four deaths in five cases) is a frightening example of technology's influence over reason. Surgeons 'had' to act because certain mechanical techniques were mastered, even though biological determinants of the transplant recipients' survival were acknowledged to lie beyond the experimenters control."

Another characteristic, *self-augmentation* of technique, can be seen in the fact that a point in technical evolution has been reached where our civilization is being transformed by technique and progresses with little—if any—decisive intervention by man. Technical progress is irreversible; it acts according to a geometric, not an arithmetic progression. The fact is that technique augments itself, because the problems it creates—for example, polluting rivers, stripping mountains, transplanting hearts—can only be solved by further development (augmentation) of technique. (p. 92) This is *the* problem of stripmining, which Harry Caudill's argument recognizes. Caudill insists that the only "solution" is to prohibit the stripping of the coal-laden mountains. To "restrict" stripmining merely augments the technical problem. Similarly, the self-augmentation of technique reveals the superficiality of the most recent political moves in this country to deal with the problems of "pollution." Liberals all, we have convinced ourselves that pollution is simply a question of good-will and . . . money! But the only "solution" to polluted rivers, atmosphere, etc., is augmentation (including bureaucratic augmentation) of the very technical developments that produced them. *Technique* cannot make polluted air, water or earth "natural" again. What replaces a poisoned nature will be a product of technique, not nature—and with it, additional technical problems which in turn are augmented by technique. Technique cannot "restore" nature, any more than the Houston Astrodome is a replication of Ebbets Field. As the story of birth control, tranquilizer, organ transplant and similar techniques makes evident, no one takes account of the new world (and in a way, new men) created by these techniques. Could we, now—after a century or two of escalating environmental pollution and bio-chemical adjustments of the human system—dare we straightway eat the products or breathe the air of technically sterilized water and atmosphere? Could fish and lobsters live in *technically* clean waters? If so, would they be safe for man formed by new environment to consume?

No one knows. Few ponder the fact that what might well emerge from haphazard, which is to say political, efforts to (in the idiom of the twentieth century) "fight" the "war" on pollution—inasmuch as it will not be "nature"—might be a series of disasters akin to the thalidomide episodes, or the early years of bio-chemical efforts at birth control (the "pill").

A third characteristic, the *monism* of technique, means that the technical phenomenon—embracing all separate techniques—forms a whole: *technique, everywhere it is applied, presents the same characteristics.* That is why it is ridiculous and useless to talk about the "use" and the "abuse" of technique; about technique for peace and technique for war (one thinks of the easy conversion of airplanes into warplanes and merchant ships into warships). "Techniques of peace and alongside them other and different techniques of war simply do not exist, despite what good folk think to the contrary." (p. 98) It is meaningless to talk about "good" police techniques. Police technique *is the same everywhere* it can be applied, by good or by bad policemen. This is why large industrial establishments, armies, political communities, educational and ecclesiastical establishments are more and more organized along the same lines: whether they are "good" or "bad" industries, armies, nations, businesses, colleges, or churches, they are all organized by technique. (We sought in *Katallagete,* Spring 1968, to direct attention to the theological significance of the Church's inevitable acceptance of the security techniques of society. See "The Church and Riot Control." The point of our example was simply that *all* institutions, especially in urban areas, become technological prisons, if they are to "survive" in the technological era. And this is true, whether they be the greatest Northern or Southern seminaries or the meanest of affluent churches. *This* crisis is the only agenda for any serious consultation on "The Church and the Future of Society.") "In a sound evaluation of the problem, it ought not to be said: on the one side technique; on the other, the abuse of it. There are different techniques which correspond to different necessities. But all techniques are inseparately united. . . ." (p. 96) "Not even a moral conversion of the technicians would make a difference," says Ellul. "At best, they would cease to be good technicians." (p. 97) Here is a critical factor in the century of total war and totalitarian politics. Why the A-bomb? Ellul provides a far more plausible account than either the New Left or the Old Warhawks: Along with other technical developments, it was necessary in atomic research to pass through the phase of the atomic bomb—a transitory but necessary stage. But why did it have to be "used" in this interim period? "Because," says Ellul, "everything which is technique is necessarily used as soon as it is available, without distinction between good or evil. *This is the principal law of our age.*" (p. 99).

(There is neither comfort nor exception to this "principal law of our age" in political arrangements such as the 1963 "Limited Nuclear Test Ban Treaty" between the United States and the Soviet Union. Rather, such arrangements confirm, and frighteningly so, Ellul's thesis about the relationship of technique to the state. I. F. Stone, in an outstanding series of articles on the politics of disarmament in the *New York Review of Books* in the spring of 1970 documents the power of technique—following Ellul's "principal law of our age"—in the military-industrial-technological complex to determine the political complex since World War II. To the point is Stone's account of "The Test Ban Comedy" [*New York Review of Books,* May 7, 1970]. Emphasizing that the "safeguards" which President Kennedy guaranteed to the Joint Chiefs of Staff were in effect a bribe for their "support" of the Treaty, Stone demonstrates conclusively that these "safeguards" "ensured an intensified arms race. The safeguards, as given by General [Maxwell] Taylor in the Senate hearings, read like a meticulously spelled-out treaty between the military and the Kennedy administration, an agreement between two bureaucratic superpowers. It proved more significant than the treaty itself." Stone himself telephoned the Atomic Energy Commission in the spring of 1970 and learned that "there had been ninety-eight U.S. tests from 1945 until the Treaty went into force on August 5, 1970. Since then, there were 210 U.S. tests, *or more than twice as many in the seven years since the treaty as in the eighteen years before it."* [Italics added]. He also cites in the same article the important story carried in the *New York Times* of June 30, 1968, quoting unnamed officials in Washington who feared that the atomic weapons production was "coming to be based more on the capabilities of the Atomic Energy Commission to manufacture them than on the actual requirements of the military.")

A fourth characteristic of technique, *universalism,* suggests that all peoples and all political communities today direct themselves on technical principles. All peoples follow the same road and the same impulse, even though they will not reach the same point at the same time. This means that technique will involve the same effects on all peoples and on all political communities everywhere. This is the point of difference between "developed" and "underdeveloped" nations. More important, however, is the fact that technique's *universalism* well-nigh guarantees the quality of political developments in the "new" nations. Their struggle to gain technologically-directed industry—which is what they *must* do in the technological era—by political deals with the technologically advanced nations insures the *universalism* of technique's import. Moreover, this ought to suggest that any "moral ascendency" rightly claimed by the former colonial peoples (here and abroad) ("the wretched of the earth") in their struggle for political freedom counts for *nothing, absolutely nothing*, in the course of their development as modern national communities. (Andrew Kopkind considers the effect on the Black Panthers when "inevitably [they] became a media event. *Ramparts* magazine built circulation on Cleaver's writings; television and the mass-circulation press inflated the Panther image and marketed it along with nudity, drugs, and rock music." *Hard Times*, January 12-19, 1970). The universalism of technique is a fundamental fact in domestic and international politics, and is guaranteed by the *monism, universalism* and *autonomy* of technique.

By the autonomy of technique, Ellul directs attention to the complete separation of the goal from the mechanism, the restriction of the technical problems to the means, not to the end, so that *for technique, the means becomes the end*. Technique cannot interfere with efficiency in any way, for any cause. Examples of this characteristic are most obvious in the direction of domestic police power in advanced technological countries, and armed intervention by these countries abroad. "It matters little whether the police action is legal, if it is efficient," says Ellul. (p. 133) This was Johnson's failure in Vietnam: Moral failure is no longer relevant politically. *Efficiency* determines both "moral" and political judgments. Had Johnson been willing (or "able"?) to obtain an efficient victory in Vietnam—and this would have meant at least: 1. Not provoking the Russian or Chinese directly against American forces; and 2. A relatively quick and decisive action, no longer than ten or twelve

33

months—he would have been regarded (as was his predecessor because of the missile crisis) a statesman-without-peer. Proof of this can be found not only in the fact that only two Senators (Morse and Gruening) spoke from the first about the "morality" and "legality" of the American invasion of Vietnam, but also in the rush of opposition which developed in the Senate and elsewhere *after* it became obvious that the United States could not win a relatively clear and cheap decision (sometime late in 1967, which the Tet offensive in the winter of 1968 only confirmed). The technical dimensions of America's policies in Vietnam—now labelled "Vietnamization" by the Nixon administration—are thoroughly covered in a most important essay by Noam Chomsky, "After Pinkville," *New York Review of Books*, January 1, 1970. Chomsky documents what seems to me the very point of Ellul's analysis of these characteristics of technique applied to strategic and tactical bombing. The bombing of North Vietnam "produced no military advantages" but was undertaken "at least in part because it was one of the things that the United States military forces were best able to do," according to then Deputy Assistant Secretary of Defense, Adam Yarmolinsky! But the decision to end the bombing of North Vietnam represented not a shift in policy, but an adjustment of tactics; in effect, the intensification of the bombing program elsewhere in Southeast Asia. The shift seeks to meet what has always been the principal fact in Southeast Asia: the base of guerrilla activities is the countryside, and to that extent difficult to control ("pacification") by the American military. The bombing and artillery policies now attempt what search-and-destroy missions sought to do, *viz.*, move the people to the urban ("pacified") areas. "So long as an organized social life can be maintained in South Vietnam, the NLF will be a powerful, dominant force," Chomsky explains. He records the tactical shift (*not* policy modification) to deal with just that fact, a shift from the American infantry to the B-52's, fighter-

34

bombers and a Vietnam "mercenary force." The policy includes an extensive use of computers and other technical apparatus in the current phase of the Southeast Asia operations. Technique forces people into the technical compounds, i.e., the cities. It seems to be working. American troops are brought home, and everyone supports the President's efforts for "peace." Moreover, the Pentagon is pacified. Chomsky quotes a speech by Army Chief of Staff William C. Westmoreland in October, 1969: "Technologically the Vietnam war has been a great success. . . . machines carry more and more of the burden."

> I see an army built into and around an integrated area control system that exploits the advanced technology of communications, sensors, fire direction, and the required automatic data processing—a system that is sensitive to the dynamics of the ever-changing battlefield—a system that materially assists the tactical commander in making sound and timely decisions.

Chomsky's article documents the details, the quality, and the consequences of this "great success."

In a related comment, Ellul argues that "the rules obeyed by a technical organization are no longer rules of justice or injustice. They are 'laws' in a purely technical sense." (*The Technological Society*, p. 133) Those who have read his analyses of the political consequences of technique have no reason to be surprised with Vietnam (or "Vietnamization") or government moves against the Black Panthers, the Chicago "conspiracy," Dr. Spock, etc. "It is now a well-established tradition of government to observe the law when nothing is happening; but if something happens, a state of emergency is declared during which special laws will be in force. This happens precisely at the moment when some group tries to use force for its own ends. At that moment the state's reaction is pitiless: it abandons the framework of the law and engages in a contest of force with the group in question until it has quelled the rebellious group and

35

made it reenter the ranks. Put differently, when the state is led by circumstances to employ force, it never observes the law, and we find ourselves in the presence of naked violence." (*The Political Illusion*, p. 74)

"As far as the police are concerned, the highest stage is reached when the legislature legalizes the independence of the legislature itself and recognizes the primacy of technical laws ('states of emergency'). True technique will know how to maintain the illusion of liberty, choice, and individuality; but these will have been carefully calculated so that they will be integrated into the mathematical reality merely as appearances." (*The Technological Society*, p. 133)

"What seems most disquieting is that the character of technique renders it *independent of man himself.* . . . The important thing is that man, practically speaking, no longer possesses any means of bringing action to bear upon technique." Man has no power or means to subjugate technique. It is a "sociological phenomenon, and in order to cure or change it, one would have to oppose to its checks and barriers of a sociological character." But whatever is of a sociological character has itself been changed by technique. "Technique is essentially independent of the human being, who finds himself naked and disarmed before it." And modern man finds only one reasonable way out: "to submit and take what profit he can from what technique otherwise so richly bestown upon him. If he is of a mind to oppose it, he finds himself really alone." (*The Technological Society*, p. 306)

These relationships between the technical phenomena and society bring man into a new environment. Specifically, Ellul insists, "from the political, social and human points of view, [the] conjunction of state and technique is by far the most important phenomenon in history"—a conjunction that can in no way be considered "a neutral fact." (*The Technological Society*, pp. 233, 247) The totalism previous states sought but failed to achieve be-

36

cause they lacked not the will, but the power, the modern state can now accomplish by the conjunction of the state and technique. "Louis XIV assumed the tone of an absolute monarch, but he did not possess the practical means to make his subjects obey his will in any well defined way." (p. 231) It is not possible here to summarize even briefly Ellul's analysis of the manner and the consequences of the conjunction of state and technique. A large segment of *The Technological Society* is devoted to a discussion of the evolution of the state's "encounter" with technique. Most significant to American cops-and-robbers-two-party theory of politics is this judgment: "No deliberate choice on the part of the state, no theoretical decision, has brought about this growth of technique; its causes were independent of the personal or collective. The modern state could no more be a state without technique than a businessman could be a businessman without the telephone or the automobile." (p. 253) This is the single most important factor which explains why and how *all* states—despite tradition or ideology—are moving along similar paths to the same destination, the technical society. Moreover, it also explains the disintegration of reform or revolutionary movements in the twentieth century: technique simply casts aside what it cannot transform to its own use. These movements of all states toward The Technical State ("the One Garrison"?), and their absorption, or the corruption, of movements for reform or revolution, are the *one* urgent subject on the agenda of the social, historical and theological disciplines. It is a measure of the nature and success of the technical society that they are not.

"Technique causes the state to become totalitarian, to absorb the citizens' life completely. . . . Even when a state is resolutely liberal and democratic, it cannot do otherwise than become totalitarian." (p. 284) Ellul's account of the disintegration of law and justice in Western society is particularly appropriate to the United States today: the superiority of overt dictatorships

37

"stems wholly from its massive exploitation of techniques. Democracy has no choice in the matter: either it utilizes techniques in the same way as the enemy, or it will perish." (pp. 288-89) Democracy *must* use "propaganda" (the subject of a separate study in his trilogy on the technological era), which by definition is anti-democratic. This, in turn, involves the administration of law and justice, and increasingly they become powers in the service of the state. ". . . In all of twentieth century Western civilization, the concept of order and security is substituted for justice as the end and foundation of law when judicial technique becomes sufficiently developed. The formula then becomes: 'Better injustice than disorder'. . . . Therefore, the law and the police are identical, for the law is no longer anything but an instrument of the state." ". . . Law insures order instead of justice . . . . [which] explains the enormous proliferation of laws." The consequences may be "reduced to two: law becomes a mere instrument of the state; and, in the end, law disappears." (pp. 295-299) Police power in all societies becomes more and more technical; when that happens, police power "assumes the leading position in the state and becomes a fundamental institution, not merely a supplementary one. It affirms itself as the 'essence of the state.' It appears as a mysterious entity which evades all laws and assumes complete autonomy. . . . In fact, we might as well have an undisguised totalitarianism which controls everything, since the simple use of techniques produces a totalitarian structure of the state, as it does in the economy." (p. 286)

The detailed examination of the conjunction of technique and the state is Ellul's *The Political Illusion.* The "illusions" are a part of the character of "the technological society." Technique has increasingly been used by, and uses the state which, in turn, assumes more and more of the function and power formerly held by individuals or institutions in society—transportation, education, care of the poor, etc. The traditional Western political processes—and the notions about them concerning popular participation and control and now in the almost universal demand that politics "solve" everything—all of these are not only incapable of dealing with and in fact exacerbate the basic problems of contemporary politics, but are themselves "political illusions" in the face of the political and social consequences of conjunction of technique and the state. The state in the technological era has the power to do, and in fact does, more and more; but as it does so, it is less able to perform the traditional functions of politics. Ellul's account of "politicization" is basic to any serious discussion of the meaning of the contemporary political crisis. Ideological debates increase in intensity at the very moment that everyone demands that everything be treated according to patterns set in the world of politics. "The nation state is the most important reality in our day," and because of the conjunction of technique and society, democratic and communist states are moving in a similar pattern. ". . . . It must be stated that *all* problems *have*, in our time, become political. It is not just a question of accepted political procedures being applied to questions that at first glance do not seem political. The point is that these questions *are* by now in the political realm, and political procedures are applied to them because they have become part and parcel of political affairs." (*The Political Illusion*, pp. 9-11. Italics Ellul's.) Hence "the modern state is *not* primarily a central organ of decision, a set of political organs. It is primarily an enormous machinery of bureaus." It gradually absorbs the citizen's life completely, so that the state, the one institution which might have served as a brake upon technique has "abdicated this function, renouncing its role in favor of technique." (*The Technological Society*, p. 305)

This, at the risk of oversimplification, is the meaning of the technological state: bombarded by the propaganda networks found in all modern states (and *all* communications are government-controlled, regardless of the formula any particular state uses to control the media), citizens are rendered incapable of true political reflection. Indeed, citizens affirm the very technical principles which ease them into the technological garrison state.

> The words the *totalitarian state* inevitably evoke clichés and passionate opinions. But these no longer represent anything but historical reminiscences. The totalitarian state we are discussing here is not the brutal, immoderate thing which tortured, deformed, and broke everything in its path, the battleground of armed bullies and factions, a place of dungeons and the reign of the arbitrary. These things did certainly exist; but they represented transient traits, not real characteristics of the totalitarian state. . . . Torture and excess are the acts of persons who use them as a means for releasing a suppressed need for power. . . . It does not represent the true face of the completely technical, totalitarian state. In such a state nothing useless exists; there is no torture; torture is a wasteful expenditure of psychic energy which destroys salvageable resources without producing useful results. . . . There is nothing arbitrary, for the arbitrary represents the very opposite of technique, in which everything "has a reason" (not a final but a mechanical reason). . . . The totalitarian state does not necessarily have totalitarian theories, nor does it necessarily even desire them. On the contrary, what we call totalitarian doctrines litter up the clear line of the technical state with aberrant elements such as "race," "blood," "proletariat." The technical state is the technical state only because it exploits certain technical means (*The Technological Society*, p. 287).

"Revolution!"? In the political sense, it is an "illusion;" a "burlesque," Ellul calls it, because revolutions must assume the very characteristics of the technical totalitarianism in order to fight the totalitarianism they seek to overthrow.

That political revolution is a "burlesque" because it offers no real alternative to technological totalitarianism is underscored by Ellul's examination of the "morality" of the technological order. (See *To Will and To Do*, pp. 184 ff.) "We are entering into a new form of morality which could be called technological morality, since it tends to bring human behavior into harmony with the technological world, to set up a new scale of values in terms of technology, and to create new virtues." This morality, Ellul finds, has three principal characteristics: it is a morality of behavior, it excludes all moral questioning because "the normal" replaces "the moral," and it makes success and failure synonymous with good and evil. In brief, he argues that the morality of the technological order "is solely interested in man's external conduct." Intentions, sentiments, ideals, ambiguities and perplexities of conscience are irrelevant—at least so long as they *remain* inward! In any case, external behavior is fixed, not by moral principles, but "in terms of precise technological rules—psychological and sociological." As the organization of all phases of human activity is perfected, the more exact the patterns of good behavior become identical with "efficiency." Fewer and fewer real choices are to be made because "the behavior for a technical world is dreadfully uniform. It obviously imposes itself upon the individual. There are not a hundred ways of employing a given technique to achieve an end." (Hence, the majority revulsion in the United States about the dress and "hair" of some of the young and, in turn, the gradual uniformity of the dress and "hair" of the young as the technological order adjusts and absorbs the manifestations of this disadjustment of the young for its own purposes.) Ellul notes the elimination or denigration of the "family virtues, good fellowship, humor, play, etc." "A man may act ignobly toward his comrades or his wife, but if he practices the virtues essential to work all is forgiven him. He is cited as an example. Most of the great heroes of our day, scientists, aviators, etc., are of this type."

It follows, therefore, that "man is no longer asked to act well, but to act normally." Technique defines what it means "to act normally." Imperatives are found through averages established by the social sciences, determined by statistics, by psychological evaluation and by generalizations of sociologists and political scientists. Adjustment is

41

the highest virtue because to be adjusted is to be good; to be maladjusted is to be evil. "The chief purpose of instruction and education today is to bring along a younger generation which is *adjusted* to this society," an insight sufficient to explain the massive support of police and National Guard violence against maladjusted students, ghetto dwellers, etc., as well as the deep emotions and enthusiasms unleashed by Vice-President Agnew's attack upon students, ghetto dwellers, etc., as maladjusted to mainstream America. Most Americans, including most young Americans, understand (or at least accept) as "normal" anything its government does in Southeast Asia or anywhere else: "As long as conduct is normal," Ellul explains, "there is no reason to reprove it in the name of morality." Presidents Johnson and Nixon validated their domestic and foreign adventures by public opinion polls, not by the Constitution or by any traditional values of humanitarianism: "It is no longer legitimate to declare good or evil that which is accepted as normal." "To act normally" explains not only the importance of the Kinsey Report which, as Ellul observes, rejected "traditional sexual morality, not in the name of objective science, but really in the name of the morality of the normal"—which is, incidentally, a much more accurate, albeit less incendiary explanation of the "sexual revolution" than is usually given by social scientists, theologians, self-styled revolutionaries and liberationists, etc. And, "to act normally" also explains the quality of the "morality" which functions as conscience or imperative in so large a majority in the United States on the crises of racism, war, politics, ghettos, education and campus unrest, "the young," law and order, drugs, etc. "To act normally" reduces the political processes to the very illusion and burlesque that Ellul has described.

What is the real horror of My Lai (called "Pinkville" by the U.S. Army in Vietnam)? Not women and babies ripped apart by the most advanced weapons of technology's arsenal in the hands of (in the words of our

42

Presidents) "America's fighting men" carrying out America's policies. Not that. We had plenty of that in the reports of scholars and newsmen and photographers reporting America's victories in North and South Vietnam and North and South Korea, the Dominican Republic, the firebombings of Tokyo, and especially in Hiroshima and Nagasaki. Any segment of these would more than equal in horror what was discovered in My Lai—although these discoveries brought few official and semi-official expressions of horror and threats of courts-martial or war crimes tribunals.

My Lai is the *ab*normal image of women and babies ripped apart at *point-blank range*, their eyes terrorized and unbelieving, staring into gun barrels and bayonet points and into the eyes of the executioners of America's policies, "America's fighting men." *That* is the horror of My Lai. Not the *victims*. The victims of Hiroshima and Nagasaki and Hanoi and Saigon were and are equally grotesque—but few if any Senators and Congressmen and silent majority Americans and their humorists suffered from boiling stomach juices when they heard about and saw the victims of Hiroshima and Nagasaki and Hanoi and Saigon. The horror—which is to say, the *ab*normality— is *how* it happened at My Lai: point-blank range, "America's fighting men" (not the savage Geronimo and his bloodthirsty redskins), terrorized eyes, mutilated babies. That is what is hard to endure and is not normal and therefore "immoral" in the technological era. To act as "they" acted at My Lai is not "to act normally." It is not to be "efficient." It does not transmit well on Huntley-Brinkley or Cronkite. It is not the "normal" action of bombers launched from the technological marvel of aircraft carriers, dispatched by radar and blessed by Bob Hope and his current symbol of "sex," and by Christ's and the Lord God's own: this is the activity that is "normal" in the technological era; we can and do and have lived with it with little demur for thirty and more years. Two miles up; two miles, that is, away from the ripped and bleeding victims, "America's fighting men" staring not into benumbed and pleading eyes of babies and pregnant girls and the old papa-sans, but peering with goggled eyes through oxygen-filled masks into the gadgets, dials, needles, buttons, switches, radars . . . . Clean . . . . Stainless Steel . . . . Color TV . . . . The normality of pastel-tiled bathrooms and Holiday Inns and Interstate Highways and 707 jetliners. The normality that we have made ourselves over into as we became adjusted by technological morality.

But perhaps the most important consequence of Ellul's analysis of technological morality is that in our day technique guarantees the moral victory of totalitarian "normality" just as it guarantees the political victory of totalitarian efficiency:

> Technology offers man a fulfillment of the good which is easy, effective, and justified in advance. Man's decision is obtained through adhering to technical progress. There can be no debate, no personal decision involved in the matter. The good is obvious. It goes along with power. There can be no question of escaping it. One will end with a perfected conformism never yet achieved in the moral sphere. In fact, never until now had morality been armed with an unassailable authority. Never before had the good been obvious and beyond dispute. Never had there been a factual identification between the good and happiness. Never had there been a coincidence between individual moral decision for the good and material social development. All this has been realized and achieved by technology. The technological good is irrefutable. It cannot be challenged. Man is moving toward a situation in which he will no longer be able to choose evil. In a certain sense, one can conceive this as putting an end to morality. (*To Will and To Do*, p. 190)

And in the end, that which is instinctive and spiritual in man is integrated by means of those techniques especially designed to "adjust" man to the technical society —education, standardized job descriptions, intelligence, vocational, aptitude tests, etc., etc. With this "final integration," Ellul concludes,

44

the edifice of the technical society will be completed. It will not be a universal concentration camp, for it will be guilty of no atrocity. It will not seem insane, for everything will be ordered, and the stains of human passion will be lost amid the chromium gleam. We shall have nothing more to lose, and nothing to win. Our deepest instincts and our most secret passions will be analyzed, published, and exploited. We shall be rewarded with everything our hearts ever desired. And the supreme luxury of the society of technical necessity will be to grant the bonus of useless revolt and of an acquiescent smile. (*The Technological Society*, p. 427)

The real problems which mankind faces in the technological era cannot even be eased by the contemporary political process. (And that is why Ellul has given up participation in "reform" movements, signing petitions, etc., etc.) But this does not mean that the crisis should be abandoned or ignored by retreats into varieties of self-serving communes, or by trying to redirect the process "from within." "Ultimately, politics obsesses us and gives us hallucinations, fixing our eyes on false problems, false means and false solutions: we must therefore leave politics behind, not in order to abandon all interest in the *res publica*, i.e., collective and social life, but on the contrary, in order to achieve it *by another route,* to come to grips with it again in a *different way,* on a more real level, and in a decisive contest." The state must not be allowed free reign and face no obstacles in its technical obliteration of man's humanity. A "rigorous arbiter" is needed to force the state to adjust itself. The dilemma, says Ellul, is either to continue the dead-end road of trying to solve the crisis created by the conjunction of technique and society with the traditional politics now transformed into "illusions" by technique; or, to abandon those illusions and create positions which reject struggle with the state, not in order to modify or reform certain elements within it, but "to permit the emergence of social, political, intellectual, or artistic bodies, associations, interest groups, or economic or Christian groups totally independent of the state, yet capable of opposing

45

it, able to reject its pressures as well as its controls, and even its gifts." ". . .It is important above all never to permit oneself to ask the state to help us." (*The Political Illusion*, p. 220)

To the charge that this proposal is "entirely utopian," Ellul answers with a statement that measures the seriousness of the crisis and the distance we are from even beginning a resolution of it:

> I have never said that it *is* possible. I have only indicated what I consider to be the basic condition for social and political life and the *only* way to escape the political illusion. If one does not want to follow it, so be it. The future is clear enough under such conditions. More or less quickly, the political illusion, which is transitory in nature, will dissolve into ashes, and what will be left will be an organization of objects run by objects. (*The Political Illusion*, p. 223)

It is here—the prospect of a future "organization of objects run by objects"—that Ellul's "compositions in counterpoint" become urgent. What was called at the beginning of this essay as his "theology of confrontation" can be seen as his deliberate effort to pit the Christian faith against the technical direction of modern society. Ellul's writings on both theology and society are his attempt to perform the task of the "rigorous arbiter," to create an awareness of the nature of the technical order, which in his judgment is the only way to permit social, or even Christian, groups to emerge "totally independent of the state, yet capable of opposing it, able to reject its pressures as well as its controls, and even its gifts."

Ellul's first work on technique was written in 1935; in 1948 he blocked out his theological and sociological tasks in *The Presence of the Kingdom*. This remains the best synopsis of his theology of confrontation between one set of covers, although forthcoming volumes of his Christian ethics may be expected to continue this type of one-volume work. Despite his own misgivings about the current usages of the phrase, Ellul remains the exponent of "revolutionary Christianity," which is the real meaning of his "theology of confrontation." As John Wilkinson observed in his introduction to *The Technological Society*, "for Ellul, *to bear witness to the fact* of the technological society is the most revolutionary of all possible acts." "The first duty of a Christian intellectual today," says Ellul, "is the duty of awareness: that is to say, the duty of understanding the world and oneself, inseparably connected and inseparably condemned, in their reality. This means the refusal to accept appearances at their face value, and of information for information's sake . . . . the consoling illusion of 'progress,' and of the improvement of situations and of men, by a sort of benevolent fatalism of history." (*Presence*, p. 118)

It is not surprising that his first exposition of "revolutionary Christianity" in *The Presence of the Kingdom* (France, 1948; United States, 1951) evoked little interest (but in places downright hostility). What he sought (and seeks) to do in this theology of confrontation is to demythologize the twentieth century in the light of the revelation of God in Jesus Christ. Specifically, this means, among other things, that he is cautious if not hostile to the church in "social action" as well as to "revolutionary" or "reform" movements which seek or require an institutional expression to oppose the problems of the technical society. And this means, in turn, a lack of interest in what is today called "the Church" (which is, today, in fact, institutions: bureaus, buildings, property, and budgets which by and large perform social and welfare functions). It brings him into the opposition of those who would "reform" this notion of "the Church" through Jonathan's Wakes, COCU's, Vatican II's, etc., etc. He goes to the New Testament, rather than sociology, for directives on what "the Church" *is*. This brings him to "revolutionary Christianity." Others— especially, of all folk, American critics!—call this a rigorous and unwarranted individualism. Ellul's case seems simple enough: given the nature of the technical world today, the work of "the Church" cannot be undertaken institutionally. The individualism—or the revolution—is one that is found in the Bible; "individualism" that "calls out" ("elects") an Amos, or Isaiah or Jeremiah; the "revolution" that begins with the confession that the Christian life begins "not because men chose Christ . . . but because Christ has chosen them." It is not because "Christians choose to go out into the world that they work there, but because Christ sends them there." This may call forth specific and concerted action, but it may just as well not. (*Presence*, p. 43) The Christian, therefore, is an ambassador: "he is the subject of another state, he is the ambassador of this state upon earth (2 Corinthians 5:20); that is to say, he ought to present the demands of his Master, he establishes a relation between the two, but he cannot take the side of this world." (p. 45)

Long before the "theology of hope" followed secular theology and the death-of-God as Protestantism's final flourishes of relevance in a world long since bored with their flourishes, Ellul explained why the Christian "is a man of the future, not of a temporal and logical future, but of the *eschaton,* of the coming break with this present world." That is the revolutionary situation into which Christ calls Christian revolutionaries: "to be revolutionary is to judge the world by its present state, by actual facts, in the name of a truth which does not yet exist (but is coming)—and it is to do so, because we believe this truth to be more genuine and more real than the reality which surrounds us." (*Presence,* pp. 50-51) These are the credentials of the Christian as revolutionary: "he is the one who already 'lives' [the return of Christ] and already makes it actual and present in his own environment." (*Presence,* pp. 49-50) The Christian leads a "style of life" which confirms what God has done for us all in Christ, and by this very confirmation he rejects and opposes the explicit dehumanizing of the technological society. (pp. 49, 50, 61) Christians, of all men, therefore, must be aware "that what actually matters, in

48

practice, is 'to be' and not 'to act' ". (p. 90) It is "not a question of doing good but of embodying faith, which is fundamentally different. It is not a question of doing works but of bearing fruit." (*To Will and To Do*, p. 217)

> It is not [the Christian's] primary task to think out plans, programmes, methods of action and of achievement. When Christians do this (and there is an epidemic of this behaviour at the present time in the Church) it is simply an imitation of the world, which is doomed to defeat. What *we* can do is of no importance unless we can offer it with a 'good conscience toward God.' (*Presence*, p. 80)

"A man who spends all his time in action, by that very fact ceases to live . . . . What matters is to *live*, and not to act. In this world, this is a revolutionary attitude, for the world only desires (utilitarian) action, and has no desire for *life* at all." (*Presence*, pp. 91-93) The history of certain Christian actions confirms this: the Christians contributed toward the ending of slavery in the Roman Empire not by onslaughts on the legal structure, but "because the Christians of the day were so conscious of their equality with their slaves, since they were all, as Christians, looking for the return of Christ." (*Presence*, pp. 84-85)

Such are the sketches already present of Ellul's vision of revolutionary Christianity in the technological society. The appearance of the first part-volume of his Christian ethics (*To Will and To Do*, soon to be followed by the French publication of the second, and concluding volume to Part One, *l'Ethique de la Liberté*) indicates that the "theology of confrontation," the "compositions in counterpoint," may occasionally be read in the same work instead of in two separate works. But, as he repeatedly emphasizes, the ethics will not be a system of morality which puts down principles for all men to follow—which protect man from God. Nor will they be a listing of imperatives—which deny the meaning of the death and resurrection of Christ. "If works are indispensable for salvation the death of Jesus Christ is rendered vain."

49

(*To Will and To Do*, p. 260) Everything the Christian does has "no meaning unless he is fulfilling the only mission which he has been charged by Jesus Christ, which is first of all *to be a sign.*" (*Presence*, p. 12. Italics Ellul's) Christian ethics therefore has specified tasks:

> What is the meaning of the fact of being liberated by Jesus Christ from the tyranny of things, and so of regaining the possibility of using them without being enslaved by them? What is the meaning of being committed by Jesus Christ in a true encounter with others, and so of regaining the possibility of serving them and loving them? What is the meaning of the fact of being enlightened by Jesus Christ concerning the destiny of the world, and so of regaining the possibility of serving God and of loving him with all one's heart, with all one's soul, with all one's mind? (*To Will and To Do*, p. 267)

And that is the task Jacques Ellul puts before all Christians, West of Eden.

TECHNOLOGY, POLITICS, AND THE CHRISTIAN FAITH

GABRIEL VAHANIAN

First, some preliminary observations:

1) From the demythologization of the Gospel to the politicization of the Church by way of the secularization of Christianity, it seems that in each case we are confronted with one and the same concern, namely: to bring the Christian faith "up to date," to bridge the gap between the Christian tradition and the "modern world." When, for example, Bultmann seeks to demythologize the New Testament, he could not do so unless the myth in question were a myth *of the past*. Unlike him, Jacques Ellul thinks that it is not the past, *but the present* that must be demythologized. To be sure, the task Bultmann set for himself may turn out to be one that does not exclude but also one that must necessarily precede Ellul's own conception of what needs to be done. And, indeed, like Bultmann, Ellul is often charged with locking up the Christian in the ultimate subjectivity of faith.

Nevertheless, the point which Ellul is seeking to make must not be overlooked: what *also* needs to be exploded are the very myths by which modern man lives, though perhaps unconsciously. These myths basically belong to

GABRIEL VAHANIAN is Eliphalet Remington Professor of Religion and Director of Graduate Studies in Religion, Syracuse University. He is the author of *The Death of God* (1961), *Wait Without Idols* (1964), *No Other God* (1966); and has written for *The Nation, Concilium, The Christian Century, Dialog, Commonweal* and other journals.

two families: that of political ideology (which Ellul exposes as "the political illusion") and that of technological progressivism or evolutionism (which mistakes the fundamental problem of man for problems which by definition can only be adjusted technically).

2) At the risk of being simplistic, one might say that there was a time when nature was more than trees and rivers, more than geography, or geology, more than an obstacle to be overcome in order to achieve some technological prowess; likewise, there was a time when history, too, was more than facts, more than a chronology of events and more also than an ineluctable process of causality. At first threatened by nature, man emancipated himself from it, and then lived and understood the experience of his reality in terms of history: God the creator was also the Lord of history. Modern man, however, can identify himself neither as natural man nor as historical man: his destiny is bound up with something like a mystique which differs radically from both of the older ones: "technique," i.e., technological society.

3) As for Ellul himself, he is hard to pin down. Were it not for his most distinctive style and its caustic effects, one could hardly believe it is the same man who has written all the books he has published to date. I make this remark not only because the range of his interests includes law and ethics, sociology and technology, as well as theology, but also because he can anticipate a theme and denounce it when it becomes a slogan. Thus, some thirty years ago when "revolution" was not a word whose resonance would appeal to Christian ears, Ellul was among the first to "listen in"; and now, just published in Paris, his latest book is entitled *Autopsie de la révolution*. Previously, his well-known *Présence au monde moderne* had already found its counterpart in *Fausse présence au monde moderne*. Not that he contradicts himself. But he does not step twice in the same river. And the result is that he will be misunderstood by the left (those for whom faith is identified with the assump-

52

tion of secular tasks and goals), and by the right (those who would isolate the faith from the concerns as well as the wisdom of this world). The risk Ellul is thus willing to run is that, dismissed by the former, he may merely end up being annexed by the latter. This article will, therefore, try to show why Ellul cannot and must not be dismissed by the left, much less annexed by the right, even if one is irritated by his neglect or at least by the absence of a cogent theological method to cope with the new problems brought about by technology. Though still mightily iconoclastic, Ellul's fideism provides us with too sketchy a theological scheme, when it does not merely call us back into the old problematic. Be that as it may, I still think that in the main Ellul is to be commended for not wavering in his sustained contention that man's self-understanding is today governed neither by nature nor by history but by technology: consequently, political ideology becomes the new illusion or the new opiate, and the concomitant politicization of the Church a dead-end if not some retrogressive panacea. In other words, technology neutralizes politics just as history once neutralized the determinism implicit in the uncanniness of nature.

THE EMERGENCE OF TECHNOLOGY AS THE NEW "MYTH"

From Nature to History.

In order to clarify the present implication of the scheme according to which Ellul thinks that the context of man's self-understanding has shifted from nature to history and finally to technology, it may be appropriate to begin by underlining what is meant by "nature." The concept of nature has a twofold connotation, which harks back to the etymological meaning of the word itself. In Latin, *natura* means "being-born-ness;" it refers to the way things are either because of their fundamental contingency or because of their no less fundamental ineluctability, their necessity. What, then, is significant from

Ellul's point of view is the way in which contingency and necessity seem to combine in the things of nature as well as in the very nature of things. Thus, the idea of man as nature refers to the way in which, once born into this world, man himself is determined by the nature of things. Progressively, however, it can be shown that the nature of things refers less and less to the *things* of nature, and more and more to man's *environment*, whether this environment may be conceived in terms of nature itself, or in terms of history; or more precisely in terms of necessity or in terms of man's contingency, that is to say his freedom.

Put differently, the nature of things refers to that specific realm of necessity by which in various epochs man has variously felt threatened and from which he has sought to emancipate himself, though only to abdicate to a new realm of necessity. Thus, at first hostile to man, nature (in Greek, *physis*) is apprehended as personifying divine forces. These forces account for both man's alienation and the process by which he tries to end his alienation through *metaphysics,* and situate himself over against the things of nature and beyond the pale of their ineluctability. The Greeks understood man as a rational animal. For Ellul, however, the chief characteristic of man is his ability to contest the way things are. This is shown in the fact that Biblical man is the man who not only de-divinizes nature, but also consecrates his emancipation from it by apprehending it as God-structured rather than self-structured, that is, as created by God. And the world on which man must depend —if only in order to attest his dominion over it—ceases to be that of nature and becomes that of history. God is the God of this history, in the light of which it will later be affirmed that in Christ there is neither Greek nor Jew.

To sum up, man contested nature by means of metaphysics and desacralized it by means of an historical conception of his God-given destiny. The things of nature will no longer determine again the "nature" of man. And we can no longer go back to the idea of man as nature or, more particularly, to the still lingering variant of this idea, namely, the notion of a natural law. Freedom, writes Ellul, "is not an immutable fact graven in nature and on the heart of man. It is not inherent in man or in society, and it is meaningless to write it into law." He adds: "reality is a combination of determinisms, and freedom consists in overcoming and transcending these determinisms."

From History to Technology.

If history was the instrument of man's disalienation from nature, it was due largely to the fact that history was understood as the history of *God's* saving acts, as eschatology. So long as eschatology was thus the ultimate frame of reference it was possible to prevent history from sacralizing itself, from becoming a mere substitute for the deterministic web of necessitarianism which the Greeks had identified as nature or as a self-contained cosmos.

It is at just this point that Ellul's critique of the present situation can most easily be misunderstood, all the more so since it just so happens that eschatology has again become the dominant theme of theology. Ellul's contention deserves for this very reason very careful attention. His thesis could perhaps best be expressed in the following manner: While it is true that eschatology is the primary category of today's theological reflexion, the fact is that eschatology is itself today understood in the light of history, *rather than history in the light of eschatology.* Not only, then, has an inversion taken place in the traditional understanding of their relationship, not only has there been a permutation of their respective roles, but the history, in the light of which eschatology is understood, is itself tributary of an ideological sacralization of the inherent meaning history is claimed to be the bearer in and of itself. Eschatology—which was to history as metaphysics was to nature—has been dissolved into political ideology. In just the same way on another level, the otherworldly has given way to the thisworldly, and the Christian era has ended in the post-Christian era. No institution, writes Ellul, can be retrieved and reinvigorated once it has become outdated. Political ideology seems to subscribe to a similar position, but tends to construe it in terms of a conflict, say, of generations, or of the left versus the right, the world versus the Church, etc., etc. Not only are institutions in themselves irretrievable, but the very nature of the successive crises for which precisely they once supplied a resolution binds the notion of history to a situation which no longer expresses that combination of determinisms characteristic of today's reality. For today's reality is predicated neither on the necessitarianism of nature nor of history, but of technology. Political ideology, Ellul's argument runs, is consequently as reactionary as was the corporatism of Christendom in its golden age.

And like it or not, Ellul has constantly and consistently argued that *"technological civilization is our new nature."* This does not imply progress, it merely means that the arena of the task by which faith assumes its call to iconoclasm has shifted. Just as history brought something new into the picture of man's self-understanding, so does technology: "primitive man, hemmed in by prohibitions, taboos, and rites, was, of course, socially determined. But it is an illusion—unfortunately very widespread—to think that because we have broken through the prohibitions, taboos, and rites that bound primitive man, we have become free. We are conditioned by something new: technological society."

Three points remain to be made in this connection. They are most easily made, first, by stressing the difference between primitive techniques and modern technology, next by refraining from identifying the latter with the machine, and finally by being alerted to the positive as well as to the negative implications of "technique."

With regard to the first point, Ellul contends that primitive techniques were, so to speak, *qualitative* by contrast with the *quantitative* nature of modern technology. More specifically, he says that "primitive techniques have no reality in themselves; they are merely the intermediary between man and his environment . . . they are subjective." What has changed is the relation between the technical phenomenon and society. Whereas primitive technology belonged to a particular civilization, today's technology has taken over the whole civilization. It has taken over all of man's activities, not just his productive activity. It reduces the industrial revolution to a tempest in a tea-pot. And thus, today's technology "transforms everything it touches into a machine . . . and integrates the machine into society." Which brings us to the second point.

This concerns the most common temptation to identify technique with the machine, electronic or otherwise. If that were the case we would still be living in the wake of the industrial revolution. But we have entered another age, into another realm, one "in which the machine itself can play no role," and in which even science becomes subservient to technology (cf. the NASA scientists protesting against mere technological prowess, and resigning). Saying that the machine plays no role becomes clearer, I think, when one realizes that while, however little, it contributed to the humanization of man, the machine may not necessarily continue to do so in the context of the new necessitarianism. Or, when one realizes that *efficiency*—in all its connotations, from the technical to the human—has been simply substituted for *decision*. Accordingly, by denouncing today's technological phenomenon as the most dangerous form of determinism, Ellul argues that "technique is the totality of methods rationally arrived at and having absolute efficiency in every field of human activity." And yet technique is in itself neither good nor bad, and with that we come to the third point.

57

Ellul's assessment of technology is both positive and negative. On the one hand, he points out that man, by realizing the full extent to which he was indeed determined (whether as a biological, or a physiological as well as a chemical organism) discovered a new way to self-determination and this way, towards man's further liberation, could well be the way of "technique." Indeed, nothing prevents technology from being the vector of a new step in the process of man's humanization. On the other hand, Ellul can also write: "The technical society . . . will not be a universal concentration camp, for it will be guilty of no atrocity. It will not seem insane, for everything will be ordered, and the stains of human passion will be lost amid the chromium gleam. Our deepest instincts and our most secret passion will be analyzed, published, and exploited. We shall be rewarded with everything our hearts ever desired. And the supreme luxury of the society of technical necessity will be to grant the bonus of useless revolt and of an acquiescent smile." (*The Technological Society*, p. 427)

POLITICAL IDEOLOGY AND THE CHURCH

Political Illusion.

What precipitates the deterioration of politics into illusion is a twofold cause: on the one hand, the historicization of eschatology which results in the *identification of history with politics*; on the other hand, the *identification of politics with efficiency.*

With respect to the first aspect of this deterioration, Ellul shows that since God has been eliminated from the driver's seat of history, political realism has in fact become a surrogate for the sense of history. Whatever history may be, it is accordingly *what takes place at the level of political action,* and as a result no action is deemed serious unless it calls for political commitment. Moreover, in the face of the dehumanizing—though perhaps only superficially so—implication of the all too sudden confrontation with a technological universe, all those who champion the primacy of political engagement much too easily or conveniently overlook the fact that the contemporary vision of politics rests on the violation of the very basis on which politics originally was founded, namely virtue. From an exercise in virtue, politics has thus become *an exercise in efficiency,* more specifically the efficiency of the organization.

If such is the case, how long must it take before we come to the realization that politics has become an illusion? Indeed, if efficiency is the criterion, then everything is permitted and man succumbs to what Bertrand de Jouvenel has called the *mythe de la solution,* to the idea that every problem by definition brings with itself its own solution. And the illusion is even more poignant when even the solution of personal problems is seen as depending upon—when *all* problems are predicated on—the organization of society or its re-organization. What, then, Ellul asks, can values be whose realization hinges on nothing other than man's own absenteeism? Indeed, if politics still is defined as the art of the possible, then such an art is more and more the monopoly of the technician.

It is because, unconsciously or consciously, they assume that technology means humanization that both the left and the right wings of politics tend to resemble one another more and more. There is no capitalism which today has not annexed this or that aspect of Marxism. Nor is there any kind of socialism which has not likewise appropriated for itself some of the ideals of bourgeois culture, such as the automobile, the washing machine, and so on. Against both the left and the right, Ellul's point is well taken: technology is not humanization but a further opportunity for it.

Not that technology merely neutralizes political ideology. Technology itself is in a way implicated in the expansion of this, today's illusion. For it "diffuses the revolt of the few and thus appeases the need of the millions for revolt." And yet, it is the same Ellul who is now rejecting the new, so-called theology of revolution or of violence. He rejects the theory of "just violence" for the same reason that he rejects the medieval theory of the "just war." By succumbing to the theory of just war, medieval Christianity succumbed to the determinism of nature. "Nature is the power to kill." That remains true, regardless of what constitutes our "nature," including technological society. Therefore, any theory of just violence will evince the same mistakes as those committed by Christendom, even though ironically enough our latter-day theological advocates of revolution, Ellul remarks, do so precisely in order to protest against that very idea of Christendom.

On this score, Ellul may be quite right. But he fails to convince simply because by virtue of his own argument he is led to appear as the champion of man as an *individual* threatened by the technological organization of society, and to advocate a theology which on his own admission will fail to convince—though the reasons why it so fails may not be those Ellul himself likes to think. For it is the world which is the sphere of faith, not the church. And though once the church was the iconoclastic evidence of the ecclesial principle of faith, the church may now well be too bound up with those institutions of the past which cannot be retrieved.

The Politicization of the Church.

It is in connexion with Ellul's recriminations against the politicization of the church, that his apocalypticism shows up the most. By saying this, I am trying to argue that Ellul is quite right in denouncing the historicization of eschatology. (His *Fausse présence au monde moderne* develops the themes of the worldliness of the church and the secularization of Christianity in discussions of "the conformation of the church to the modern world" and "politicization of the church.") But he is wrong in construing eschatology in what could only be considered as apocalyptic terms: *Agapé*, Ellul argues, cannot inspire any political action. Therefore, he claims, to construe politics as an extension of the commandment of love is to rob the Christian's presence in the world of its intrinsic significance. To say that Christ is the *lord* of the world without confessing that he also is its *saviour* is for Ellul today's greatest temptation; it is today's apostasy. For, he says, it is not the church that needs to be renewed so much as the world. Ellul, however, seems to disregard the fact that the two must be linked. The reformation of the world (*mundus semper reformandus*) may well continue to be the first obligation of the Christian today; it will not take place, however, if the church is not also reformed (*ecclesia semper reformanda*). True enough, the presence of the kingdom is presence in the world only to the extent that it is the presence of that which is not of this world. It all depends on where the emphasis falls: whether on the presence or on that which is not of this world, on commitment to God or on involvement in the world. It seems to me that ultimately Ellul disjoins the two, and does so under the pretext— a valid one, mind you!—that faith is a matter of personal decision, while technology and ideology rest on efficiency, that is, on a notion of "happiness without any real basis for it." But, then, what can a personal decision still mean, when in order to make it, its agent need no longer descend in the arena of life?

That Ellul himself also wonders about this problem is evidenced by the following quotation: "Our man of the golden age, therefore, will be capable of 'happiness' amidst the worst privations. Why, then, promise us extraordinary comforts, hygiene, knowledge, and nourishment if, by simply manipulating our nervous systems, we can be happy without them? The last meagre motive we could possibly ascribe to the technical adventure thus vanishes into thin air through the very existence of technique itself." (*The Technological Society*, p. 436)

In the last analysis, Ellul's predicament is the same as

Martin Niemoeller, who writes: "First, they put the Communists and Jehovah's Witnesses in the concentration camps—but I was not a Communist or a Jehovah's Witness, so I did nothing. Then they came for the Social Democrats—but I was not a Social Democrat, and I did nothing. Then they arrested the trade-unionists—and I did nothing, because I was not one. Then they arrested the Jews—and again I did nothing because I was not a Jew. Then they came for the Catholics, but I was not a Catholic and I did nothing. At last they came and arrested me—but then it was too late already."

Indeed, the ultimate question is whether the Son of Man will find faith on earth when he comes back. But is it *still* a question, Ellul would like to add, if one forgets that, like the manna in the desert, faith cannot be hoarded?

THE SOCIAL THOUGHT OF JACQUES ELLUL

CHRISTOPHER LASCH

Although Jacques Ellul has written on theology, law, and many other subjects, he is known in the United States principally as the author of three sociological studies: *The Technological Society, Propaganda,* and *The Political Illusion.*[1] These works alone, however, convey an imperfect impression of the force and originality of Ellul's thought. What is valuable in his social writings takes on meaning only when one considers the ethical, cultural, and philosophical position they are intended to support. In itself, Ellul's analysis of modern society is unoriginal (except for one or two sharp insights) and in some respects even misleading. Moreover, the work for which he is best known, *The Technological Society,* is the weakest of his three sociological treatises, although it is also the most ambitious. In large part, it repeats what has already been said by Max Weber, by Veblen, and by theorists of the managerial revolution, the "new class" and "mass society."

Modern history, in this view, is the history of the rationalization of all phases of existence. Politics and statecraft, subjected to the requirements of technique, become autonomous processes unamenable to democratic control. Knowledge ceases to serve a critical function,

CHRISTOPHER LASCH is Professor of History, University of Rochester. He is the author of *The American Liberals and the Russian Revolution* (1962), *The New Radicalism in America* (1965) and *The Agony of the American Left* (1969). He has contributed to *The New York Review of Books, The Nation,* and *Katallagete.*

since the demands of technique lead thinkers to make "a hard and fast separation between what is and what should be," dismissing the latter as subjective and therefore unscientific judgments of value. New methods of propaganda and thought-control are developed to a high degree of efficiency, ensuring the continuing domination of technology. No longer the master of his destiny, man is reduced to an object, and society evolves inexorably toward a bland totalitarianism—a "worldwide totalitarian dictatorship," in Ellul's words, that "no obstacle can stop."

The bleakness of its pessimism distinguishes *The Technological Society* from its predecessors in twentieth-century sociology. Its central thesis does not. Neither does Ellul's attack on Marx, which draws heavily on conventional misrepresentations of Marxian theory.[2] Since the attack is directed not against Marx but against a caricature of his ideas, Marxian analysis of modern society is not seriously challenged by *The Technological Society,* any more than it is challenged by other theories of mass society. George Lichtheim once said of Weber's sociology of religion, hailed as a great conceptual breakthrough by Weber's admirers, that the entire elaborate structure "fits without difficulty into the Marxian scheme." The same holds for Ellul's theory of the "technological society." It is not for this that Ellul commands our attention.

His other works are another matter. Of particular importance, in my opinion, are *The Political Illusion,* the recently published *Violence,* and a very early work, *The Presence of the Kingdom,* which anticipates most of the writings that have followed it. Published in France in 1948, *The Presence of the Kingdom* appeared in the United States in 1951, but received little notice. Only with its reappearance in paperback in 1967 did it obtain a wider reading public. By that time all three volumes of Ellul's sociological trilogy had appeared in English translation. Yet the earlier book supplies the moral and philosophical underpinnings of Ellul's later writings. Short and clear, it seems to have been written at white heat. "In my description of the contemporary scene, behind each bare statement lies an experience; and I could support each statement with concrete examples. To do this, however, would require more leisure than my present circumstances permit, for the time is short." (*Presence*, p. 138) Modern society rushes toward a disaster that only revolution—"a radical transformation of our present civilization"—can prevent; yet that same society is characterized by a "profound immobility," and "incapacity for revolution." (p. 35)

The Presence of the Kingdom is addressed to Christians, but it raises questions that all radical intellectuals have to confront, whether or not they approach them from a Christian perspective. The crisis of the faith is one aspect of the cultural crisis of our time, and Ellul's plea that the church speak directly and critically to social issues springs from the same concerns that have led other intellectuals, working from secular premises, to insist that culture must no longer be pursued as an activity having no relation to politics, that artists and scholars must abandon the pretense of neutrality, and that a new humanism, in short, is likely to take shape only if it makes connection with the struggles of exploited classes to change the world. In the years since *The Presence of the Kingdom* first appeared, pleas for culture to be "relevant" have once again become common and even fashionable; but as the level of political militancy rises, the advocates of cultural "commitment" have more and more retreated to the position they held in the United States in the thirties and which they have never ceased to hold on the European left—namely, that cultural radicalism means that intellectuals should enlist in the proletarian revolution (now seen as a global uprising of the non-white, colonialized peoples). Ellul's work, taken as a whole, constitutes a sustained critique of this position, all the more effective, in some ways, for its being cast in religious terms. When the newly militant church places itself at the service of "the revolution," Ellul believes that it ceases to bring anything specifically Christian (unless it is a particularly offensive type of sentimentality) to the understanding of modern society. Already foreshadowed in *The Presence of the Kingdom,* this theme in Ellul's thought emerges with great clarity in a most recent book, *Violence,* which was written in direct response to new-style Christian militants who argue, in the words of Richard Shaull, that the church "cannot stay out of the revolutionary struggle."[3] Ellul objects to this view on the grounds that it substitutes an appeal to the emotions for analysis and "confuses [the reader] as to the difference between socialism and revolution." He also points out that "to say that the Christian must participate [in revolutions] is to make revolution a value, even in a sense an absolute value"—in which case there is no longer any need for Christianity, all its own values having been subsumed under revolution. (*Violence,* p. 53) "Obviously, revolution is the overriding value, therefore the main argument; to be a revolutionary is more important than to be, or not to be, a Christian." (p. 54)

When Ellul himself exhorts the church to become "revolutionary," he does not mean that the church should place itself under the moral leadership of the proletariat or of any other revolutionary class. His reservations about revolution are strengthened by the knowledge that in the past—and especially in the recent past—revolutions have not brought about the liberating and democratic changes that were to have justified their violence, terror, and suppression of opponents. Ellul's writings have always reflected a profound disenchantment not merely with advanced capitalist society in the West but with its socialist alternative. That capitalism and socialism are essentially identical is one of the constant themes of his work. "At bottom, the U.S.S.R. obeys the same

66

rules as the U.S.A." (*Presence*, p. 36) This idea leads Ellul into serious mistakes, as I shall try to show later, but it does enable him to escape the illusion, so common among modern revolutionaries, that a change in political structures, without an attendant spiritual or cultural transformation, will bring about a genuinely democratic society. Ellul is one of the few contemporary radicals fully to grasp the cultural dimensions of the twentieth-century crisis. The most impressive passages in his books are those in which he speaks of people's helpless bewilderment in the face of mass communications, the assimilation of science to technique, the degradation of art, the collapse of values. His analysis of modern communications is brilliant. He shows how the mass media subject people to a barrage of disconnected and therefore meaningless facts and how this makes critical reflection on politics impossible. "News succeeds news without ceasing. For instance, in the columns of the newspaper he will read one day about an affair which quickly disappears from the paper, and also from the brain of the reader. It is replaced by others; it is forgotten. A man gets used to living like this, without a present and without a past. He gets used to living in complete incoherence . . ." [4] (*Presence*, p. 101) In *Propaganda*, Ellul explores in detail the disastrous effects of mass communications.[5]

Neither science nor art provides any alternative to the prevailing chaos. On the contrary, science and art contribute to it: science, by divorcing itself from philosophy and becoming merely a higher branch of technology; art, by giving up any pretense to make statements about objective reality, thereby dissolving in "self-expression." Neither science nor art any longer communicates anything except, in the one case, information required to solve technical problems—and even this is conveyed in symbols accessible only to specialists—and in the other case, inner experiences uncommunicable by definition. Modern art, by opposing to technological domination a

67

cult of the irrational, "guides us in the direction of mad-
ness." (*Technological Society*, p. 404) Faced with ramp-
ant disorder, men take refuge in the great "explanatory
myths" of our time: "the bourgeois myth of the Hand of
Moscow, the Socialist myth of the Two Hundred Families, the Fascist myth of the Jews, the Communist myth
of the anti-revolutionary saboteur." (*Presence*, p. 102)
These provide the only "means of intellectual coherence"
in a world made meaningless by loss of continuity, loss of
memory.

II

"In no other civilization has man been so totally re-
pressed." (*Presence*, p. 77) Unlike Herbert Marcuse,
Ellul does not refer to the repression of libido. His vision
of liberation is altogether different from that of the
"Freudian left," which proposes to free man from all
forms of external authority. Ellul holds the old-fashioned
idea that order and authority are necessary and even
desirable; that conflicts with authority are a necessary
part of education and of growing up in general; and
that "there is no liberty," as he puts it in *The Political
Illusion*, "except liberty achieved in the face of some
constraint or rule." (p. 212) When he speaks of repression, Ellul refers to the manipulation of the citizen
by the media and by the state, the destruction of private
life, the subjection of every aspect of life to the requirements of the "social machine," as defined by those in
charge of it. (*Presence*, p. 78) Ellul's conception of the
cultural revolution that would be necessary to put an
end to these forms of domination has little in common
with the conception that prevails today, which derives
not from Christian humanism but from Marcuse, Reich,
Zen, Bob Dylan, the Beatles, astrology, witchcraft, and
the occult. Ellul's perspective on culture enables him to
see the modern obsession with personal liberation as itself a symptom of pervasive spiritual disorder. *The Presence of the Kingdom* ends with a plea for "a new style

of life," since Ellul recognizes that a moral doctrine has power only to the extent that it creates a culture suited to the needs of those to whom it is addressed—in this case, the "proletarian" mass man. (p. 145) Elsewhere Ellul speaks of the need for groups of the faithful to find a way "to live on the edge of this totalitarian society." (*Presence*, p. 60) But his insistence on the need for privacy, order, and continuity ("every achievement, however humble it may be, is worthy of being preserved"); his praise of the family coupled with an attack on those who "reject love as a conflict or insist that the woman should ultimately be the same as the man"; and his belief that institutionalized tension should be clearly present in human affairs and that it is precisely the "adjustment" of all tensions that signals the approach of the "unitary society"—all this sets Ellul apart from those cultural radicals who seek escape in drugs, sexual liberation, and communal living arrangements. (*Presence*, p. 56; *Political Illusion*, p. 215) Without disregarding their positive contributions, he sees that such solutions do not seriously menace the existing order. "It is good for city dwellers to go to the country. It is good that a marked eroticism is wrecking the sclerotic traditional morality. It is well that poetry, thanks to such movements as surrealism, has become really expressive once more. But these phenomena, which express the deepest instinctive human passions, have also become totally innocuous. . . . It is harmless to attack a crumbling middle-class morality." (*Technological Society*, pp. 416-7; see also *Commonplaces*, pp. 4-8) The ruling class itself has come to believe in the need to transcend the "archaic cultures [that] still corrupt human life"; and it announces its own emancipation from the "metaphysical and dogmatic mentality" by declaring that "all doctrines which draw their inspiration from abstract conceptions have already betrayed their fundamental incapacity to organize the human world." (*Technological Society*, p. 414, quoting Alain Sargent in *The Sciences of Man Re-estab-*

lish His Supremacy) What can the cultural left, with its worship of direct experience and its revolt against reason, add to this indictment of humanist culture?

In his latest book, *Violence,* Ellul addresses himself directly to the hippie phenomenon. His idea of cultural renewal takes on additional clarity in contrast with that of the hippies. Their "splendid élan," he writes, "seems doomed from the start, because the hippies have no understanding of what their real place in society is." Attempting to challenge the technological society, they are in fact supported by it. "In reality, they are only the product of its luxuriousness." Moreover, they offer a diverting escape from boredom. "The hippies introduce color, youth, pleasure. To be sure, they are a bit shocking, but a society held together by boredom is more or less proof against shock." (Pp. 120-21) This is particularly the case when so many of the values of dissident cultures merely reaffirm, in extreme form, those of the surrounding cultures: subjectivity, the impossibility of verbal communication, salvation through technology (drugs), utopia as the absence of tensions and conflicts.

When Ellul speaks of the need for a "moral revolution," he clearly has in mind something quite different from either hippie nonviolence or revolutionary militancy. (*Political Illusion,* p. 224n.) The "moral revolution" does not consist of investing contemporary politics with passionate moralism. The only moral attitude toward politics, according to Ellul, is one of severe realism—one that tries to assess the probable consequences of political actions. Moralism interferes with this by contributing to the escalation of rhetoric; in the end, it merely provides additional fuel for the propaganda machine. In *The Political Illusion,* Ellul writes:

> . . . [T]he insertion of values into the discussion of political acts is never more than just words. Liberty, justice, the right of peoples to self-determination, the dignity of the human person—these are no longer anything but pale justifications

for social conformity. . . . Once invoked, they only serve to support an already existing political design. They become part of the propaganda apparatus . . . (p. 94)

It suits the interest of the state to induce in the citizen a heightened state of political passion, and nothing serves this purpose so well as moral rhetoric, whether it comes from the state or from dissident movements themselves. Unlike many theorists of mass society, Ellul does not see political quiescence or "apathy" as the chief characteristic of the mass man. The mass man is "immersed in the immediate present, disoriented, incapable of true political reflection," but he by no means necessarily lacks political opinions. (*Political Illusion,* p. 75) On the contrary, his opinions may sweep him into political engagement; he may become a militant partisan of some cause. But militancy only adds to the already overheated political atmosphere, and the violence to which it so easily leads helps to legitimize the counter-violence of the state. The absence of genuine tensions in the "unitary society" does not at all preclude violence; the recognition of this is one of Ellul's most brilliant insights.

Our French society has become a unitarian society from which tensions are practically excluded, or, more precisely, only one form of tension exists—political tension. . . . I know the reader will retort: 'What more internal tensions do you want in a country than those we have already experienced! Tension between collaborators and the Resistance from 1940 to 1945 (with all its sequels), tension between French and Independent Algeria, between army and nation, between the OAS and the anti-fascist Left . . . we live in terrible and permanent tension, and cannot see that it is fruitful.' The problem is that the conflicts we know today are exclusively of a *political* order. . . .

[T]hese tensions, of which so much is being said, and which are tragic for us because every twenty years they must be paid for with human lives, are the more tragic because they are absurd and illusory. The only tensions that still exist are political tensions, but despite their hard and violent character, despite widespread commitment to them, despite some peo-

71

ple's seriousness in the debate, they are false tensions, emptying into a void, dealing with nothing serious in the structure of our society, and incapable of producing any solution or basic innovation. (*Political Illusion*, pp. 220-21)

It is precisely because so little of real importance is at stake that political controversies generate such rhetorical excesses: there is no limit to what people can say, since their words have no lasting consequences. True, they sometimes have immediate consequences of the most appalling character; yet nothing changes as a result.

III

In what sense is politics "illusory"?

Ellul insists that the most important questions in life are not political questions; the illusion, then, lies in supposing they can be solved by political means. I think Ellul pays too little attention to the ways in which the distribution of wealth and power influences every other question. He does not regard the ownership of the means of production, for example, as an important question. That seems extremely short-sighted; but at the same time it has to be conceded that the left has raised this most important of political questions in a form that could hardly be better calculated to *conceal* its importance. Instead of arguing that socialization of the means of production is one condition essential to the survival of civilized relations among people, the left has presented it as the end of history as we know it, the end of conflict, the beginning of utopia. The trouble with this kind of thinking is that it discourages any action or reflection in the meantime; all questions are dissolved into questions of political strategy: what steps are necessary to bring about the revolutionary apocalypse, after which universal love shall prevail? In this sense it is certainly true that modern politics raises no important questions. And in a deeper sense it is true that the most important questions of all—for instance, those concerning "the interplay between constraint and liberty"—are not political and lose something—everything—when stated in political language.

For Ellul, the most serious moral and social issues revolve around relationships—parent and child, man and woman, teacher and pupil, man and God—in which there is an irreducible element of tension. In modern society, however, tensions are banished from all realms but the political. Thus in education, "the contemporary orientation is that the child must learn without pain, that it must have agreeable, seductive work, that it must not even notice that it is working, and that in class the teacher must be really a sort of game leader, a permissive leader with whom there is no conflict." But to assert that there should be no conflict between teacher and pupil "radically falsifies the child's participation in social life and keeps his personality from developing." It is just this conflict through which the pupil learns and grows, providing, of course, that "in this conflict the teacher knows that his role is not to bully, crush, or train children like animals. . . ." (*Political Illusion*, p. 211)[6]

When he cannot banish tensions altogether, the modern man translates them into political terms. What is currently happening in American education affords an excellent example of the point Ellul is trying to make. Rebelling against the blandness of permissive education, American students—and students in other countries as well—have succeeded only in politicizing the relation between student and teacher. In the new situation thereby created, every pedagogical question becomes a matter for negotiation, and bureaucratic machinery has to be created for this purpose—the very proliferation of bureaucracy that some students began by attacking as unnecessary and oppressive. Although the student protest originates, at least in part, in an awareness that education has become an empty ritual, students find it difficult—given the exclusively political vocabulary

73

in which discussion of conflicts, in our society, is invariably cast—to identify the source of the trouble as the teachers' abdication of moral and intellectual authority. They themselves accept the prevailing view that relations between students and teachers should be free of conflict and that whatever conflicts do exist therefore have to be removed or regulated by political means. The existence of conflict, in a society where conflict has been defined as exceptional and undesirable, automatically becomes a political question to which political categories—injustice, exploitation, authoritarianism, "the student as nigger"—are applied. The students hold up as an educational ideal the "free university" in which students set the standards, pursue their studies without having to be judged by their teachers, and confront their teachers, in short, as intellectual equals. To the degree that academic life falls short of this ideal, students seek political machinery to regularize conflicts by limiting what they perceive to be the arbitrary powers of the faculty. Because it has become so hard to imagine forms of authority that arise not from the wish to dominate or exploit but from inherent inequalities between teachers and students, students perceive authority in political terms and attack their teachers, not for having so little confidence in their ability to teach anything and for showing so little commitment to the intellectual life, but for acting like "authoritarians" by denying students the right to "participate in the decisions that affect their lives." The student protest thereby reinforces the flabby permissiveness of American education, since most faculties are all too willing to accede to student demands with a great show of democratic good feeling—just as most middle-class parents, in the similarly politicized struggles that take place in the home (and in many cases serve as the preliminary to the struggles now taking place in the university), have found it easier to bargain and negotiate with their children than to uphold ethical standards in a chaotic world.

The relations between men and women offer another example of the politicization of every aspect of life. Formerly the sexual relation was regarded as a private one belonging to the realm of love and therefore immune from the intrusion of sanctions derived from the realm of power. Feminism represented, among other things, an attempt not only to democratize the relations between men and women but to get rid of conflicts by denying their biological basis. Feminists did not confine themselves to attacking discrimination against women in the public sphere or to limiting the legal powers of husbands—powers that were, indeed, highly arbitrary and that gave rise to a thousand injustices. Pushed to its furthest limits, the logic of feminism denied that biological differences between men and women were of any importance and maintained, therefore, that whatever conflicts originated in those differences could be eradicated or at least regularized through appropriate political means. Thus feminists proposed to reform the family so as to eliminate sexual roles or, when that proved impossible under existing conditions, to abolish the family altogether and to assign its child-rearing functions, which allegedly interfered with the economic independence of women, to the community. That the new system may provide a more "efficient" way of ordering sexual relations and of rearing children is not the issue; what matters is that feminists have always rested their case on those grounds. One hears of the Israeli kibbutz, for example, that the advantage of the new arrangements is that the child sees his parents only in an "affectional" context, whereas toilet-training and all other matters pertaining to discipline are entrusted to the socialized agencies of child-raising. The family is thereby spared the terrible conflicts, Oedipal and otherwise, that arise when affection and discipline are concentrated in the same individuals. At this point, however, one has to ask with Ellul whether it is not precisely the conjunction of love and constraint that enables a child to grow up and to accept the constraints of adulthood without losing the capacity for love. It is true that children do grow up in the kibbutz and in fact develop into remarkably "well-adjusted" adults; but it is just that, their "adjustment" and their "ability to work well with others," so highly prized in the kibbutz, that may provide an ominous foretaste of our future.[7]

IV

Ellul sees the expansion of the private realm as a necessary defense against the tyranny of the political, but this does not mean that he wishes individuals to retreat into purely personal consolations. He is well aware that this is a "suicidal solution." (*Presence*, p. 103) When he argues that "a private vision" has to be the basis of political realism and that "private life itself must be re-established," he means something quite different from the search for personal fulfillment that indeed, in the form of compulsive consumption, pervades our highly politicized society. (*Political Illusion*, p. 205) The "privatization" of life is quite consistent with the politicization of everything. Ellul proposes instead "to create positions in which we reject and struggle with the State, *not* in order to modify some element of the regime or force it to make some decision, but, much more fundamentally, in order to permit the emergence of social, political, intellectual, or artistic bodies, associations, interest groups, or economic or Christian groups totally independent of the state, yet capable of opposing it . . ." (*Political Illusion*, p. 222) In this way he hopes that it will be possible to restore "an autonomous vitality to certain parts of society"—for instance, by creating "an authentic new tension between the intellectual and political realms." (p. 223) These words clearly imply a defense of the existing autonomy, and an attempt to enlarge the autonomy, of such institutions as the family and the school, in the face of all pressures to politicize them. They do not imply, however, that people should pretend that what happens in those institutions has no bearing on larger social questions—that intellectual life, for example, has nothing to do with politics. Ellul is not advocating political quiescence. The reason for restoring the autonomy of civil society is precisely that this "would make possible a political life that would be something else than mere illusion." (*Political Illusion*, p. 223) Ellul realizes, moreover, that the search for a new culture "is necessarily a corporate act" and that isolated individuals cannot "follow this path." (*Presence*, p. 149)

In one of his latest books Ellul addresses himself at one point to American readers who might be tempted to interpret his attack on "the political illusion" as an attack on every form of political action, or to misread his condemnation of the Soviet Union as a defense of free enterprise. He writes: "*I absolutely do not say that capitalism is better than socialism. I firmly believe the* contrary. *I absolutely do not say that defense of the poor through socialist movements is wrong. I firmly believe the* contrary." (*Violence*, p. 32) He wishes only to show that socialism and Christianity, in his words, are not the same thing—that revolution cannot be regarded as a value in itself. When he criticizes socialism, Ellul is criticizing one form the "political illusion" has assumed, whether one looks at the socialist regimes in the Soviet Union and elsewhere, at revolutionary movements in the West, or for that matter at those social democrats (particularly conspicuous in France) who have wholly assimilated the technocratic and managerial point of view and condemn capitalism only because it embodies certain lingering technological inefficiencies.

Nevertheless I think that Ellul's position would be much clearer if it were not so firmly rooted in the theory of the "technological society." In itself, the attempt to anchor moral and cultural perspectives in a hard-headed sociological analysis of modern society should elicit nothing but our admiration. It is precisely this attempt that

77

makes Ellul's work interesting in the first place; without it, Ellul would be only another moralist.[8] My quarrel is not with Ellul's long excursion into sociology, which was entirely proper and necessary, but with the particular sociological conclusions he has arrived at, particularly in *The Technological Society*—the work, as I have said, for which he is best known in the United States.

I have already referred to Ellul's hostility to Marxism, which he sees merely as one of the great myths of the twentieth century—those "explanatory myths" that explain nothing. There is no doubt that Marxism as a social movement—as distinguished from a theory of industrial society—has acquired many of the features of a mythology and that Ellul's reservations on this score have to be taken seriously. In *The Technological Society*, however, Ellul tries to ground these reservations in a counter-theory of the modern social order which tries to show that "capitalism did not create our world; the machine did." (p. 5) Here he attacks Marxism not as a revolutionary myth but as a body of analysis. Marxism is useless as analysis, according to Ellul, because the character of industrial society derives not from capitalism but from technology. In order to make a case for the decisive influence of the latter, he has to dispose of the objection that technique is a neutral force and therefore compatible with a variety of social systems, and that what matters is the class relations, deriving from production, that ultimately determine the uses to which technique is put. Much of *The Technological Society* is devoted to this task. Ellul tries to show that technique is "autonomous" and that wherever technological habits of thought come to prevail, they drive out every other consideration. For that reason it makes no sense to distinguish between technology and the use that people make of it. "In a sound evaluation of the problem, it ought never to be said: on the one side, technique; on the other, the abuse of it." (p. 96) Since every technical process is explicitly designed to solve a specific technical problem, there is

78

only one appropriate use to which it can be put. "A man can use his automobile to take a trip or to kill his neighbors. But the second use is not a use; it is a crime. The automobile was not created to kill people, so the fact is not important." In other words, the fact that cars are not used for killing—not intentionally, at any rate—does not prove that men can make a moral use of technology if they so choose and that in the last analysis, therefore, it is "man who decides in what direction to orient his researches." On the contrary, "a principal characteristic of technique . . . is its refusal to tolerate moral judgments." (pp. 96-7) It is inevitable that the same society that expends vast amounts of technological knowledge in prolonging life or in making it more comfortable will also perfect ever more efficient techniques for destroying it. The automobile and the hydrogen bomb are parts of the same social process, and it is impossible to choose one without choosing the other.

To put it another way: "There is no difference at all between technique and its use. . . . The use of the automobile as a murder weapon does not represent the technical use, that is, the one best way of doing something. Technique is a means with a set of rules for the game. . . . There is but one method for its use, one possibility." (pp. 97-8) Like much else in *The Technological Society,* this argument seems curiously removed from everyday reality. If one considers the automobile a little more broadly, not just as a machine but as part of a total system of transportation, it is apparent that in advanced capitalist society the automobile is in fact, if not a murder weapon, an instrument of violence in its social effects. Especially in the United States, the human need for open space, clean air, and livable communities is systematically subordinated to the automobile's need for parking garages and superhighways; and these things occur even though the automobile strictly speaking is designed for transportation, not the destruction of cities. This situation does not arise because the automobile in its technical aspect requires the suppression of other forms of surface transportation and thereby forces urban life to organize itself around cars to the exclusion of almost everything else. It is capitalism, not technology, that requires these things. The automobile may be designed for one use and one use alone, but this fact in itself does not explain why the state, not only in America but increasingly in western Europe as well, has chosen in effect to subsidize the automobile industry (as well as the airlines) at the expense of other forms of transportation—and this in the face of the terrible consequences to which such a policy gives rise.

V

It cannot be claimed that a system of transportation organized around cars and planes is intrinsically more efficient than a system in which various forms of rail transportation would also play an indispensable role. It cannot even be claimed that the existing system derives, as might first appear to be the case, from the unquestioned superiority of airplanes over trains. Since airports have to be built far from the center of cities, and since the only access to these centers is over highways choked with cars, travel time between the major cities of the eastern seaboard, say, is not appreciably reduced by substituting air travel for surface travel. Even from a purely technical point of view, it would make more sense to restore an efficient system of rail transport than to continue to build airports and highways that will be obsolete by the time they are completed. (It is precisely this anticipated obsolescence, however, that makes them attractive.)

City and regional planners have proposed just such an alternative system of transportation. They point out, not only that railroads are more efficient than airplanes for local and regional travel and for the transport of goods, but that the existing system has social by-products too important to ignore; that is, it contributes to the destruction of cities, to suburban blight, and to the general "environmental crisis." Yet there is no indication that the ideas of these planners will prevail. On purely technical grounds they ought to prevail, quite apart from other considerations. No one listens, however. What accounts for this anomaly?

In part the answer lies in the rise of the aircraft industry, nourished by war.[9] Obviously the aircraft industry wields great economic and political power. Yet precisely because it depends so much more heavily on military spending than on its ability to dominate the domestic market, the aircraft industry cannot be regarded as the decisive element in the American transportation system. The decisive element is the automobile industry, which is, indeed, the heart of the American economy.[10] Not airplanes but automobiles, buses, and trucks have reduced the railroads to bankruptcy and thereby destroyed their ability to compete with the airlines. The central question, then, is why the automobile industry has come to dominate the entire economy, and political life as well.

There are several reasons, none of which can be attributed to technique. First is the automobile's apparently insatiable appetite for roads, parking garages, gasoline, roadside establishments of all kinds, and innumerable ancillary goods and services. No other industry has such seemingly unlimited capacity to stimulate so wide a range of other industries. In a consumer economy the automobile plays a role analogous to that of the railroad in a nineteenth-century economy oriented around heavy industry. In the second place, the automobile has established itself as the most appropriate and glamorous symbol of the consumer culture and the values it embodies: personal mobility and the private satisfaction of culturally induced needs and wants. But above all, the automobile industry is central to the American economy because it has developed to such a high pitch the deliberate planning of waste. The industry maintains itself not only by building obsolescence into the product in the form of shoddy workmanship but by deliberately inducing changes of fashion and taste. The success with which the industry early made the annual change of models a national ritual showed how advertising could be used as a form of propaganda—a means of sustaining an ideology and a culture organized around compulsive consumption.

Ellul is well aware of the metamorphosis of advertising into propaganda, but he does not see that the origins of this·process lie not in the expansion of the state but in the need to make mass culture an adjunct of corporate planning—of the planned production of waste. It is true that the state plays a much larger role in the modern economy than it formerly did and that it has come to wield frightening powers of destruction. But the nearly total subjection of the cultural apparatus to the advertising industry and the corporations ought to alert us to the fact that the growth of the state has come about to serve the needs of the corporations, not to serve technology in the abstract. The relationship between the corporations and the state, moreover, is one-sided. The corporations relegate to the state activities on which the corporate system depends but which are unprofitable, while retaining for themselves the revenues created by the elaborate system of state regulations and subsidies. The state directly or indirectly trains scientists, technicians, and skilled workers; administers and finances welfare programs; sponsors urban renewal in the interests of the real estate developers and automobile manufacturers; subsidizes the huge amount of scientific research required by advanced technology; and grapples unsuccessfully with the sheer physical removal of ever-accumulating waste. But the profits made possible by these and similar public expenditures—above all by war—accrue to the corporations, while the state depends on taxation for its revenues. This one-sided interdependence of the corporations· and the state leads to the much-discussed disparity between private affluence and public squalor—a characteristic feature of advanced capitalism which, however, is never mentioned in *The Technological Society*.

Faced with dwindling markets and the threat of chronic overproduction, mature capitalism increasingly depends on imperial expansion abroad and on the domestic production of goods that will be quickly superseded. "The capitalist system lives and thrives by waste." [11] I have confined myself to the automobile industry because it is one of the best examples of this tendency, because it illustrates more clearly than others the social consequences to which it leads, and because Ellul himself introduces the example of the automobile in order to prove that technique obeys its own laws and "refuses to tolerate moral judgments." It would be possible, however, to cite many other examples of the importance of waste—the youth market, for instance, which has attained its present position in advanced economies largely because it is highly susceptible to changes of fashion and taste—and it would be possible, in every case, to show that the social disasters that Ellul attributes to technique are more accurately attributed to the distinctive character of advanced capitalist production. This emphatically does not mean that all the evils of the modern world can be charged to capitalism or that socializing the means of production would inaugurate the golden age. But it does cast a great deal of doubt on an interpretation of modern history that treats capitalism as "only one aspect of the deep disorder of the nineteenth century"—a disorder that originated in the triumph of technology. (*Technological Society*, p. 5)

VI

It is no answer to say that socialist countries are coming more and more to resemble capitalist countries in their use of propaganda and other totalitarian controls, as if this demonstrated the transcendent character of technique. This argument pays no attention to the historical setting in which socialist regimes have come to power in the modern world. It can be argued that a socialism of abundance in countries with firmly established traditions of political democracy would look very different from socialism in Russia, China, Algeria, or Cuba —economically backward countries in which political democracy has never taken firm root. It can be argued further that Western intervention in the twentieth-century revolutions in backward countries played some part, if not a major part, in forcing those regimes into an authoritarian mold—for instance, by saddling them with a debilitating arms race. These arguments do not excuse Stalin's crimes against the Russian people, the suppression of freedom in Hungary and in Czechoslovakia, or the liquidation of political opponents wherever socialist regimes have come to power; nor are they meant to do so. They do raise the question of whether socialism in backward countries is inevitably the same thing as socialism in advanced countries. The alleged identity of socialist and neo-capitalist regimes rests on a mechanical determinism that takes no account of historical variations.

The more extravagant claims made for this determinism—for instance, that it represents an alternative to Marxian theory—melt away under analysis. Deprived of these claims, the theory of the "technological society" offers insights either that are already present in Marxian theory or that fit into it without difficulty. Managerialism is merely the current version of capitalist ideology. If socialist countries share certain features with advanced capitalist regimes—and Ellul in any event has greatly exaggerated their similarities—that does not mean that there is an underlying identity between capitalism and socialism and that technique transcends both; it merely reflects the degree to which socialist regimes in undeveloped countries have had to draw on bourgeois models of industrialization. Given the shortage of technical personnel in undeveloped countries, reliance on bourgeois resources is inevitable. To conclude from this that socialism challenges capitalism only on the grounds of its technical inefficiency (*Technological Society*, p. 81) and that the most advanced elements among the bourgeoisie, indeed, have already conceded the argument and embraced socialism because it promises technically better results (*Commonplaces*, pp. 18-20), makes it very difficult to understand why those very elements have resisted with such vigor and success the spread of socialism in the rest of the world.[12]

The global struggle between socialism and capitalism, of which Vietnam is the latest and bloodiest phase, cannot be understood as a kind of factional dispute within the managerial class or, on the other hand, as the expression of mass antipathies whipped up by propaganda. At times Ellul pushes his critique of political illusions and propaganda to the point of saying that *all* politics are illusory. It is true that "the creation of political problems out of nothing is one of propaganda's most astonishing capabilities," but it does not follow that every political problem is the creation of propaganda. (*Political Illusion*, p. 213) Ellul claims that it was "American anticolonialist idealism," presumably reinforced by propaganda, that forced the Dutch out of Indonesia and the French out of Vietnam, and that American involvement in southeast Asia, therefore, "is the direct consequence of their action in disarming France." (*Violence*, p. 90n.) This account ignores several things. It was not the United States but Ho Chi Minh that "disarmed" France; far from urging the French to leave Vietnam, the United States tried to maneuver them into staying; and in fact the United States refused to sign the Geneva agreement because it did not want to be a party to the "disarming" of France. The main lines of American foreign policy have been clear and consistent: when the European powers were no longer able to hold the line against colonial revolution, the United States leaped into the breach. An interpretation that attributes all this to propaganda and "anticolonialist idealism" sacrifices historical accuracy to the internal consistency of a beautiful design.

Ellul's technological determinism adequately explains neither the structure of advanced capitalist society nor the foreign policies to which it gives rise. But the weakness of the social theory on which Ellul has tried to base his moral and cultural position does not undermine the position itself. At its best, his work helps us to make an indispensable distinction between the idea of socialism and the transcendent political myths that have been invoked to prove its moral necessity and/or its historical inevitability. His is the most thorough and convincing attack I know on the position that "revolution is *prerequisite* to reconciliation"—or if one prefers to state the issue in non-theological terms, that revolution is the prerequisite of cultural regeneration, of a genuinely civilized society. (*Violence*, p. 73) Ellul does not deny that there may be oppression that can only be ended through revolution; nor does he deny that revolutionary violence can sometimes clarify issues or create disorder "out of which (depending on how fluid the situation is) renewal may issue." (*Violence*, p. 133) What he does insist is that revolutionary violence must not be confused with the *creation* of order. Violence belongs to the realm of necessity; it is part of the natural order of things, whereas the proper object of politics is "the creation of a stabilized universe, an artificial universe (artificial in the sense that it is made by the skill of man), in which man recognizes forms and objects, assigns names and places, and creates a continuity with the help of (but also against) the fluidity of the universe." (*Violence*, pp. 91, 127; *Political Illusion*, p. 53) Out of violence, on the other hand, only chaos issues.

It must be emphasized that Ellul condemns violent revolution (while recognizing its inevitability in some situations—inevitability and justice are not the same), as a man of the left. "[I]f I attack the left in its common-places, that does not mean I am against the left. On the contrary, it is because I believe in values that only the left has stated, elucidated, and partially adopted (without acting on them), because the left has sustained the hope of mankind, because the left has engaged in the struggle for justice, that I cannot tolerate the absurdity of the present left . . ." (*Commonplaces*, p. 21) Such a position is difficult to understand for those who believe that to criticize the left is an "objectively" reactionary act. Because Ellul does criticize the left, and because he denies the primacy of politics, many radicals will regard him as a traitor to their cause. The real betrayal, how-ever, is the radical intellectuals' subordination of intellect to political passions.

NOTES

1. *The Technological Society* appeared in 1964 in a transla-tion by John Wilkinson. It was followed in 1966 by *Propaganda*, translated by Konrad Kellen and Jean Lerner, and in 1967 by *The Political Illusion*, in Kellen's translation. All of these books were published by Alfred A. Knopf.

2. According to *The Technological Society*, the last chance of revolution disappeared in the nineteenth century, when the revo-lutionary movement ceased to oppose technology with "spiritual forces" and adopted the materialist perspective as its own, thereby hastening the final triumph of economic man. "Proudhon and Bakunin had placed spiritual forces in rivalry with the economic order. Against them, Marx upheld the bourgeois order of the primacy of the economic . . ." (*Technological Society*, pp. 222-3) In an earlier work, *Présence au Monde Moderne*, Ellul devoted several pages to this "mutation of the revolutionary idea." "Proud-hon, affirming the supremacy of the human will over human con-

ditions, calling man to struggle against his situation, is revolutionary, while Marx, who explains that inevitably, by the evolution of facts (including the simple fact of man) by the play of dialectical materialism, Socialist society will emerge from Capitalist society, is anti-revolutionary." (*Presence of the Kingdom*, p. 39)

Technique, Ellul complains in another context, has "emptied socialism of any content." (*Technological Society*, p. 246) The same might be said of some of his own writings. Marx never propounded any such thing as "dialectical materialism"—that was the contribution of Engels, who sought to establish the scientific credentials of Marxism according to the positivistic standard of scientific truth that had come to prevail at the end of the nineteenth century. Marx was not a determinist; he did not deny the element of human will in history; he made no easy assumptions about the inevitability of progress; nor did he equate social progress with technology. In order to extol Proudhon and Bakunin —whose ideological heirs in the twentieth century Ellul himself would later attack—and to dismiss Marx as a thinker whom it was not necessary even to consider, Ellul first had to set up a caricature' of Marxism; or rather, had to take over the caricature of Marxism already current not only in bourgeois and managerial circles but, unfortunately, in some socialist circles as well—particularly the French Communist party. Given the level to which much twentieth-century Marxism has sunk, it is not altogether surprising that a thinker of the stature of Ellul should feel no obligation to acquaint himself with Marx's writings at first hand. His own writings, however, are the worse for this omission.

3. The quotation from Shaull, cited in *Violence*, p. 53, comes from Shaull's "Revolutionary Change in Theological Perspective" in John C. Bennett, ed., *Christian Social Ethics in a Changing World* (1966). Shaull also contributed a lengthy essay on revolution to Carl Oglesby's *Containment and Change* (Macmillan, 1967). There he attempts to qualify his position by arguing that "the most authentic revolutionary is one who can unite full commitment with a certain degree of detachment, who can keep a sense of humor that allows him to laugh at himself, and who can maintain a critical attitude toward all revolutionary thought and action." (*Containment and Change*, pp. 245-6) But this is mere rhetoric. How can "full commitment" coexist with "a certain degree of detachment"? Either one is fully committed to revolution or one is committed to some other value. It is hardly necessary to add that Shaull's essay reveals none of the "critical attitude" to revolution that he recommends as standard equipment for the "authentic" revolutionary.

4. The following succession of front-page headlines in the Chicago *Sun-Times* amply bears out Ellul's point about the com-

plete absence of continuity in the media's treatment of events. Dec. 10: "9 in Congress ask Nixon for Hampton quiz"; Dec. 11: "Mitchell reveals Mafia rule of big IRS group"; Dec. 12: "Massive tax-reform bill passed by Senate 69-22"; Dec. 14: "Supreme Court stiffens Southern school edict"; Dec. 15: "Nixon talk today: more Viet troop withdrawals"; Dec. 17: "Budget of $842 million is voted by city council".

5. See my review in *The Nation*, April 4, 1966.

6. "Just because he is superior," Ellul continues, "[the teacher] must know how to limit his own force in relation to that of his adversary—that is what is at the core of true pedagogy." Cf. the critique of education as technique and the discussion of Montessori in *Technological Society*, pp. 346-7.

7. Bruno Bettelheim, *The Children of the Dream* (Macmillan, 1969), pp. 262 and passim. "[T]he kibbutzniks' hope was that by sharing nothing but pleasure with their children, the oedipal ambivalence of love and rejection would be avoided, indicating a fear of deep attachments pure and simple, of which ambivalence is a necessary part." Part of this fear, Bettelheim thinks, can be traced back to a misunderstanding of Freud, with whose works the founders of the kibbutz movement were familiar: "Freud's analysis of the oedipal situation was misunderstood to mean that parents should never have any but good times wih their children." (p. 36) The same fear of ambivalent attachments, based in part on the same misunderstanding of Freudian theory, can be seen in the middle-class American family today, and children brought up under the new regime to which it has given rise seem to show some of the same characteristics that Bettelheim—mistakenly, I think—ascribes exclusively to the kibbutz: a strong attachment to the peer-group; a marked fear of being alone; more or less complete alienation from the past (since "there is no permanence in human relations except with the peer group" [p. 97]); a strong concern with personal "authenticity" in relations with others, unmediated by conventional forms of politeness (p. 74n.); and a lack of introspection and of a highly developed inner life (pp. 122, 130, 171).

8. *The Presence of the Kingdom* states explicitly that "what we need is to find the true structure or framework of our modern civilization." Ellul regards the position hastily sketched out in that book as no more than "a prologue to more extended study which would examine the problem of our present civilization from every aspect . . ." (Pp. 121, 137)

9. The dominance of air power in modern warfare, incidentally, does not rest on its technical efficiency. Experience with strategic bombing has shown again and again that its military effects are vastly overrated. The airplane is not necessarily the most efficient

method of mass destruction, but it is the most *expensive* method of mass destruction. That is its great advantage from the point of view of advanced capitalist society—a society, that is, which thrives on the production of unnecessary commodities. War, obviously, is the purest form of waste, and aerial warfare is the most wasteful method of war. Planes are expensive to maintain and to replace; vast amounts of money have to be spent on training those who service and fly them; but in spite of this, bombing is necessarily imprecise and its effects on civilian morale not nearly so damaging as commonly supposed, so that the entire effort is out of all proportion to the actual military gain. Bombing is also the most impersonal form of destruction, and this commends it to people who wish to murder at a safe and sanitary distance; but the aversion to other forms of murder could doubtless be over-come if considerations of corporate profits made it necessary to do so.

10. In other capitalist countries it is coming to have the same importance. In Sweden, for instance, Volvo is the largest industrial corporation.

11. Louis Boudin, *The Theoretical System of Karl Marx* (Chicago, Charles H. Kerr, 1920), p. 246.

12. In fairness it must be noted that although Ellul holds the questionable view that "the dominating ideology everywhere [sic] is a socializing, anti-colonialist ideology" or, stated more modestly, that "the socialist mood is dominant among Christian intellectuals in Europe," he recognizes that "the opposite is the case in the United States." (*Violence*, pp. 66, 72)

THE REVOLUTION: REVISITED

JULIUS LESTER

Revolution. We use the word because it tells us what we are about (those of us who consider ourselves revolutionaries/radicals/fellow travellers). It means the destruction of the system (capitalism) and the replacement of it with a new one (socialism). No one questions this. Indeed, it is the one thing all revolutionaries agree on though hardly anyone agrees on exactly how to do it.

But, what if we were wrong. Suppose that the overthrow of the existing system (and its subsequent replacement) was not the way to make a revolution. Suppose that we actually made a revolution and found that nothing of essence had changed—that we had not created the humanistic society all of us want, but had merely exchanged one exploitation for another.

We have unquestioningly assumed that our basic premises are correct: capitalism, racism and imperialism (the contemporary Apocalyptic Three Horsemen) are the ills which beset us. We assume that we have found the cure for those ills—revolution, the destruction of the Three Horsemen (and their horses?). These assumptions

JULIUS LESTER is the author of *Look Out Whitey! Black Power's Gon' Get Your Mama* (1968), *To Be A Slave* (1968), *Revolutionary Notes* (1969), *Black Folk Tales* (1969), *Search for the New Land: History as Subjective Experience* (1969) and is completing a study and anthology of the writings of W. E. B. DuBois. He is a regular contributor to *Liberation* and *Katallagete*, conducts a radio program on WBAI, the Pacifica Foundation station in New York, and teaches black studies at the New School for Social Research. He is a former Field Secretary for the Student Non-Violent Coordinating Committee.

are so commonly and uncritically accepted that it is depressing these days to talk to a revolutionary or read a radical newspaper or magazine. It's like putting a dime into a Coke machine. Never once do you get a grape or orange soda. Always Coke. To ask a radical a question is no different than asking Richard Nixon a question. Both answers are monotonously predictable, both in content and rhetoric. But, if the label on the record says Beethoven's Fifth, you don't put it on the phonograph expecting to hear Bob Dylan.

Perhaps it is time to question the basic assumptions. ("Why? We know what's wrong." "So, nothing will be lost by making sure." "It's just a waste of time." "O.K., but suppose it turns out that it wasn't a waste of time. Suppose that some of our assumptions are wrong. Then, we gain by finding that out." "Bullshit! The fascist pig power structure never changes. Power to the people and Death to all counter-revolutionaries who try to subvert the people's struggle!" Bang! Bang!) We must never think that defining the problem once is defining it for all time. Definitions must be constantly examined and re-examined. We must have the courage to look and destroy all which is inadequate for the task to be done. We ourselves must have the courage to change, to endure *la noche oscura* not once, but again and again and again.

It appears that the black and white radical political movement of the sixties has reached a point where it lacks the courage to look at itself and ask questions. It substitutes doctrine for creative thinking, conflict for tension, militancy for courage. It refuses to engage in the process of self-doubt and whenever one refuses to consider (even for the sake of discussion) that he may be wrong he increases the possibility that he might be.

Space does not permit a full explication of the development of the radical political movement of the sixties. (The reader is referred to the August-September 1969 issue of *Liberation* magazine for articles on the history of the movement of the sixties by Carl Oglesby and this writer and also this writer's *Search for the New Land* published by Dial Press.) But as that movement developed, two separate aspects of it became apparent by late 1968—the political and the cultural. Though there was much over-lapping between the two, they were different enough in essentials to make for two distinct approaches to solving the problems America faces.

The dominant organization of the radical political movement is the Black Panther Party. It is the dominant organization in the black community more by default than accomplishment, because no one else is as well-organized or visible. It is supported by blacks not so much for what it represents itself to be—the "vanguard" organization—but because it is being attacked by 'the man.' Within the white radical political movement, the Black Panther Party is accepted as the "vanguard" and thus it has become the leader of the radical political movement. (How this came about will be touched on later.)

The BPP and its white supporters have defined the essential root of our ills in classic political terms—capitalism. It is the polluted fountainhead from which all else has proceeded and the solution is obvious: destroy capitalism and institute socialism. Because it is an all-black organization, it recognizes racism as an evil, but maintains that racism is the child of capitalism and exploitation and will die when the parent dies. That is logical. Just as 2 plus 2 being 4 is logical. Unfortunately, history cannot be reduced to simple addition, or even complex equations. Political organizations and individuals (among others) have always imposed a logic and structure on history in an attempt to give it the appearance of order. Thus, history becomes the logic, the structure, and the order which may bear absolutely no relation to how people have lived their lives. (Man has also imposed a logic, structure and order on the rising and setting and subsequent rising of the sun, called it "time" and measured it out in one second intervals of ticks and tocks.

93

Thus, man lives by his wristwatch and not by the rising of the sun.) History, Marxist or otherwise, gives a very limited picture of a nation or a civilization and absolutely none of people. But this limited picture is thought to represent the totality of human experience, and how it is interpreted determines one's politics. Because the BPP uses a Marxist interpretation of history, it refuses to consider the possibility that capitalism is not the root of America's problems, that racism may not magically disappear with the demise of capitalism and coming of socialism. Their politics is one of a massive confrontation between the forces of good and the forces of evil, and, since mankind is moving toward the bright sun of socialism, the revolutionary forces will achieve victory and mankind will march forward into the brighter tomorrow. When pared to its essentials, it is a politics which bears a resemblance to a Western movie, where the good guy (who sometimes, like the Lone Ranger, dresses in black and rides a white horse) meets the bad guy and always wins. (Note for a future essay: The philosophical similarities between the medieval morality play and the politics of confrontation.)

At the other end of the spectrum are the black youth culture (cultural nationalists) and white youth culture (hippies). The former is concerned with a return to blackness, to the cultural roots, to achieving and sustaining an identity separate from the dominant white culture. The objective is either the eventual creation of a black nation or the destruction of the system. There is much over-lapping between black political and cultural radicals. There is more agreement between them on the necessity to destroy the system; however where the BPP would say that this is to be followed by socialism, the black cultural radical wants a black nation. Whether it is to be socialist is unclear. (Ameer Baraka [Leroi Jones] has been working on the concept of communalism.) The black youth culture sees the primary problem facing black people as racism, not capitalism. The oppressive

94

and exploitative nature of capitalism is recognized, but the black cultural radical maintains that oppression on the basis of race is more insidious and immediate. The black political radical acknowledges the truth of this, but says that racism cannot be dealt with under capitalism. (This is linear thinking, tending toward cause and effect kinds of analyses.) The BPP insists that the conflict beween races is embodied in the class struggle; the cultural radical considers the conflict between races (a synonym for cultures) to be independent of the class struggle. The BPP sees a class struggle at work in the black community; the cultural radical would admit this, but seeks to subvert it by appeals to unity on the basis of race. (Note for future essay: The role of nationalism in the thought of Ho Chi Minh.) The black cultural radical views a class analysis as being applicable to white people and considers it a serious mistake to think that ideologies evolved by whites for their problems can be applied uncritically to blacks and black problems. They would agree with Senegalese President Senghor, one of the architects of Negritude, who faced the same problem, though in a slightly different context.

> Our error was not that we fought with the weapons of colonialism . . . but with the weapons of Europe. *To fight colonialism we borrowed the weapons of the European proletariat, who told us that their struggle and our own were identical.* Similar, perhaps, but not identical, for our situations are not the same. . . . In fact, the European proletarians are held in a dependent status as individuals grouped in a class, not as a race or a people. As for us, we have been colonized, to be sure, as underdeveloped, defenseless individuals, but also as Negroes. . . In other words, as people of a different race and different culture. . . . (Italics in original. Quoted in Irving Leonard Markovitz, *Leopold Sedar Senghor and the Politics of Negritude*, p. 86.)

The cultural radical looks at himself and the world through the eyes of a black man who is oppressed. The political radical looks at the world as one who is oppressed and happens to be black. The difference is important, because it determines where each focuses his attention.

The cultural radical begins with himself as the matter to be changed. Although he seeks the destruction of the system, he does not organize, propagandize or agitate *directly* toward that end. His immediate concern is legitimatizing and institutionalizing blackness in his own mind and those of other blacks. Black pride, black self-knowledge, and black separatism are his focus. (These elements can also be found in the thinking of the Urban League and Southern Christian Leadership Conference, but more as adornments which are necessary to be even listened to by blacks today. For the black cultural radical, blackness is the core, the quintessence of existence.) This leads to getting rid of one's slave name and adopting an African one, to black studies, black poetry, theatre, African dress, Afro hair-styles and a complete withdrawal from whites. (One can have everyday physical contact with whites, on a job, for instance, and still be in a state of total withdrawal from them.) The cultural radical wants nothing from whites, whom he equates with the system. He knows that because he has changed himself, the system must either change to accommodate his change, or it must try to destroy him. There is no doubt in his mind which solution will be attempted. Thus, he comes together with the political radical to study guerrilla warfare, weaponry, karate and prepares for Armageddon, which, for the cultural radical, will bring the total elimination of white people from the face of the Earth and Instant Paradise.

The black political radical, who was more than likely a cultural radical at one time, recognizes the value of black pride, etc. However, black culture for him is only a weapon in the struggle and it is to be subordinated to the revolution. Its correct use is as a means of raising the political consciousness of the people and preparing them to fight. In other words, its principal value is as

96

propaganda; it has little or no intrinsic value. Because of the cultural radical's self concern (personal self and racial self are one for the cultural radical), the political radical sees him as a threat to the revolution. The BPP refers to cultural radicals as "pork-chop nationalists," and criticizes them for being self-indulgent about things which are ultimately irrelevant.

The basic point of conflict between the two is their attitudes toward whites. (The previously quoted passage from Senghor is dealing in essence with the question: How do we relate to whites?) The political radical, with his class analysis, is not anti-white. The cultural radical wants nothing to do with whites. The political radical is fighting for all oppressed people. The cultural radical is concerned solely about black people. The political radical addresses himself to all people on the broadest level, while working specifically with blacks. There is only one level for the cultural radical—black people the world over. Finally, the political radical says there is no answer until the system is changed and he takes power. Thus, all of his energies and activities are directed toward that end. The cultural radical says that by changing himself he is forcing the system to change; he wants a black nation. If it can come into being under capitalism, fine. If not, fine. But the cultural radical does not see destruction of the system as his major objective. The position of the political radical implies that responsibility for his condition lies outside of himself. The position of the cultural radical implies that the cause of his condition may lie outside, but the condition will only be changed from inside. This is very explicit in the writings of the two most prominent black cultural radicals, Ameer Baraka and Maulana Karenga. The political radical marches into a church and demands reparations for black people. The cultural radical says it is the responsibility of the black community to redress its grievances, not to demand (which is militant begging) from whites. Malcolm X, in defining black nationalism, set forth what has

97

come to be the basic direction of the black cultural radical.

> . . . black nationalism . . . is not designed to make the black man re-evaluate the white man—you know him already —but to make the black man re-evaluate himself. Don't change the white man's mind—you can't change his mind, and that whole thing about appealing to the moral conscience of America—America's conscience is bankrupt. . . . We have to change our own mind. . . . We've got to change our own minds about each other. We have to see each other with new eyes. We have to see each other as brothers and sisters. We have come together with warmth so we can develop unity and harmony that's necessary to get this problem solved ourselves. (*Malcolm X Speaks*, pp. 39-40)

The cultural radical, and Malcolm X was no exception, has not been able to decide, however, whether he should concentrate totally on doing solely for himself, as Elijah Muhammad has done with the Nation of Islam, or whether he should first destroy the system. He feels that an injustice has been done to him and quite naturally wants revenge, wants to make America pay. Thus, he vacillates between the two. More and more, however, the cultural radical is concentrating his energies on changing the minds of blacks about each other and less on white people (and all of their attendant concerns).

The white youth culture bears a surprising resemblance to the black youth culture, though not in specifics. The resemblance comes from the fact that the white youth culture also starts with self (individual) as the source to be changed and not the system. In fact, the white youth culture, like its black counterpart, has been involved in a new definition of self. Through drugs, rock music, communal living, sex, and sensory experience, it has rejected society's definition of self and is in the process of creating its own. It also seeks to be as separate as possible from the dominant society. It recognizes that the society needs changing, but prefers a cultural solution of the problems, not a political one. (Cf. The

Beatle's song "Revolution.") The way to change society is to change people's heads, for everyone to just go ahead and "do his thing."

The result of the black and white youth cultures has been a massive transformation in the consciousness of black and white youths regarding themselves. And this is what makes these cultural phenomena qualitatively different from practically any other occurrence in American history. Hundreds of thousands of blacks and whites (millions, in fact) now see themselves as separate from the dominant society, but not on the basis of alienation (the social disease of previous generations), but on the basis of creating a new community, of being a part of a new community. They have changed themselves within the existing political framework and have thereby created tensions within the existing framework—tensions which threaten the existence of that framework.

This is not to say that the black and white youth cultures have discovered the road to Utopia. They are limited in their scope, but less than the black and white political radicals in theirs. The black cultural radical seeks salvation in black culture, failing to recognize that the separateness which existed between the culture of the colonizer and the colonized in Africa was almost complete (except for the black educated elite and those tribes, like the Ibos in Nigeria, who were selected by the colonizer for the role of native colonizers). The degree of separation was far less here. Where it was possible for much of African tribal life to be culturally unaffected by colonialism, black life in America has been subjected to the same societal forces as white life. Albeit that the amalgamation of these forces with black culture had a different effect than it did on whites, sometimes the existence of these forces cannot be ignored. All too often, black cultural radicals think that blackness has made them immune to any of the forces from which whites suffer. This is a tragic mis-calculation. There is also a tendency for cultural radicals to be self-indulgent, as black political radicals maintain. A daishiki, ultimately, is still just a piece of cloth, not the Holy Grail.

The white youth culture, while representing an alternative life-style, has to depend on the dominant society for its existence. It can exist at the fringes only because America is so affluent. What will happen to this culture as its adherents get older remains to be seen. The white youth culture's emphasis upon "doing your own thing" is potentially self-destructive, for doing one's thing can mean ignoring what is being done to others. And the role of drugs in this cannot be under-estimated. (A horrifying example of the weaknesses of the white youth culture occurred this past December at an open-air rock festival in California where the Hell's Angels murdered an 18-year-old black youth on the stage in full view of 400,000 members of the youth culture. No one lifted a finger or raised a voice. They were "doing their thing," as were the 39 New Yorkers who heard the screams of Kitty Genovese in the night were doing theirs when they refused to help and refused to call for help.)

So: the present radical movement offers a political and cultural definition and solution of society's problems. Of these, the political seems to be the more obvious at present. Its principal concerns for the past year or so have been the Vietnam war (white political radicals) and the physical oppression of the black community (black political radicals). (The black cultural radicals have been involved in black studies; the white cultural radicals have been creating communes, rural and urban.) The dominant organization has been the Black Panther Party, which is supported unquestioningly by white political radicals and most white cultural radicals. The BPP's rhetoric and public posture (more than its program) have led it into increasingly bloody confrontations with the police, culminating in the year-end murders of Fred Hampton and Mark Clark in Chicago. This was inevitable, proceeding logically from the definition of the

100

struggle articulated by the BPP. If the problem one is facing is physical (capitalist oppression), then the means to solve it must be physical (violent revolution). The problems of the people resulting from this physical oppression are also defined as (solely) physical—hunger, poor housing, poor medical care. Therefore the solution is also physical—free breakfast programs for children and free medical clinics. There is no question that the physical needs of people should be met. However, is the best way to meet those needs through physical (material) means? As long as the problems are defined as physical ones, there is no other solution available except a physical one. This is not to say that the physical problems (poverty, inadequate medical care, etc.) do not exist. They do. However, are they the only problems which face our society? If not, what are the other problems? Do they proceed from capitalism (as the political radical tells us)? If not, from what do they proceed? Can they be solved by the destruction of capitalism and the creation of socialism? And finally, can, in actuality, the physical problems be best solved by physical means?

Everyone is aware of the overwhelming role that technology plays in our society. It is impossible to imagine existence without it and though many have pointed to the dangers of a technological society, we accept it because of the material benefits. We are aware, in vague ways, that a technological society is dehumanizing. (Capitalism is only physically oppressive; the profit motive may have led to the assembly line, but it is the assembly line, a primitive technique, which is dehumanizing, not the profit motive.) But we think that there is nothing wrong with technology; only the way in which it is used. Jacques Ellul in *The Technological Society* seeks to prove the contrary. Technology, he maintains, is an independent force, functioning according to its own nature without regard for political ideology or economic system. Technique ("a standardized means for attaining a predetermined result") exists

101

outside and above race, nation and the principals which that nation uses to order its society. "Technique has taken substance, has become a reality in itself. It is no longer merely a means and an intermediary. It is an object in itself, an independent reality with which we must reckon." And we are scarcely aware of it. Theodore Roszak in his *The Making of a Counter Culture* observes that "it is characteristic of the technocracy to render itself ideologically invisible. Its assumptions about reality and its values become as unobtrusively pervasive as the air we breathe. While daily political argument continues within and between the capitalist and collectivist societies of the world, the technocracy increases and consolidates its power in both as a transpolitical phenomenon following the dictates of industrial efficiency, rationality, and necessity." (p. 37)

Because technique is "transpolitical", it is the grossest of errors to think that a change in ideology will mean a qualitative change in the effects of technique. Ellul prefers the word "technique" to "technological" because technology is only one aspect, one manifestation of technique. Technique is that attitude of our society which places the greatest value upon efficiency, no matter what the operation or endeavor. In other words, technique is "means and the ensemble of means." The end is irrelevant. Indeed, there is no end except the means. Technique predominates in government, economics, propaganda, publicity, and every other sphere. (See Joe McGinnis' book, *The Selling of the President* for a documentary study of how technique was responsible for the election of Richard Nixon.)

One of the frightening characteristics of technique is its ability to multiply itself. Example: ". . . to make housework easier, garbage-disposal units have been put into use which allow the garbage to run off through the kitchen sinks. The result is enormous pollution of the rivers. It is then necessary to find some new means of purifying the rivers so that water can be used for drinking. A great quantity of oxygen is required for bacteria to destroy these organic materials. And how shall we oxygenate rivers?" And on and on and on it can go. Technique regenerates itself because it functions relative to what is possible, not to what is needed or moral. The atomic bomb was built because it was possible to build it. If something can be done, then it should be done, says technique. (On a less harmful level it is the attitude of technique which says, men climb mountains because they are there. A man *should* climb a mountain because he likes to, or because he wants to see what the view from the top is like.)

Because technique is concerned with making real the possible, it cannot care about consequences. One example will suffice. It is taken from the November 24, 1969 issue of *U.S. News and World Report.*

> The World Health Organization sent DDT to Borneo to kill mosquitoes. It worked fine. But it didn't kill roaches, which accumulated DDT in their bodies.
> Lizards which lived in the thatched huts ate the roaches. The DDT slowed the lizards.
> Cats then easily caught the lizards. But the cats died. . . .
> With the cats gone, rats came, carrying a threat of plague. And with the lizards gone, caterpillars multiplied in the huts, where they fed on the roof thatching. Then the roofs started caving in.

Because technique is a system carried to its logical end, its effect on man is to make him less and less necessary in any but the most functionary way. (The logical end of technique is to make man unnecessary except as a robot repairman.) Within technique anyone can be trained to do any job, because the jobs of technique do not require decisions as much as they require an ability to read dials, interpret the data and feed it into a computer, which makes the decision. Man, as a human being, ceases to exist. He becomes a function. It is Ellul's prediction that "man will . . . be confined to the role of a recording device; he will note the effects of tech-

103

niques upon one another, and register the results." Nowhere has this been more apparent than in the much publicized and very boring trips to the moon. The astronauts observed the dials and computers and reported the information back to Mission Control where more dials and computers were being observed and reported on. It was the dials which told them what button to push and when to fire what rockets and for how long. Robots could have easily commanded Apollo 11 and 12. (Before each space trip, *Life* magazine has articles on the astronauts who will be going into space. Each article tries to convince the reader that these men are human, because they have wives, children and like to play golf. There is no such thing as an astronaut with personality is all the articles prove.)

Technique exists outside morality. In fact, it creates its own morality, which is to insure its existence. As Ellul points out, any technician who tries to impose morality on technique simply ceases to be a good technician. It is impossible to be moral and go to work everyday and make napalm. Either one does not make napalm or one does and justifies it by saying that he is doing his job, i.e. doing what technique demands, as opposed to work to get paid. (Note to self: Re-read Hannah Arendt's "The Banality of Evil" in the light of technique.)

Technique exists within the radical political movement. A system (Marxism-Leninism) is thought to be the answer to a system (capitalism). Man can be organized into societies, but it is only within the past three or four centuries (perhaps beginning with the slave trade?) that it was believed that Man could be systematized. And because Man has become systematized, the aim of society thereby becomes, not Man, but the system and the preservation of it. Allegedly, the system is to be preserved, because it best allows man to fulfill his creative potential. (Each system says this of itself, be it democratic, fascist or socialist.) Thus, it becomes all important to preserve the system. ("The Technical Man

104

. . . is committed to the never-ending search for 'the one best way' to achieve any designated objective.") Because technique is 'transpolitical,' it means that "today all peoples follow the same road and the same impulse."

The end result of technique, as far as the individual is concerned, is his utter and complete dehumanization. He becomes a technician and not a human being. And all the while he is being told (and convinced) that he is free, that he is human.

Propaganda, Ellul's next book, concentrates on technique in one particular area. I will not delve into it here, except to say that Ellul once again avoids political quarrels and ideological arguments and sees propaganda functioning the same under capitalism and socialism with the same result—the creation of technicians and then reconciling them, through propaganda, to their lost humanity.

Ellul's most relevant work to one who has been in any way politically active is *The Political Illusion*, for that is what Ellul considers politics to be—an illusion. He who uses political means to solve political problems is only going around in a circle.

It is good when someone says to you, "Everything you say is a mere illusion. It has no relationship to any reality except that which exists in your head." This is what Ellul says in *The Political Illusion*, as he analyzes the basic political precepts of the twentieth century. For example, political involvement.

> In other eras, a man could be regarded as being committed by being involved in the structure and the collective life of his society—in the arts, science, religion, etc. He is no longer considered 'committed,' however, unless the implications of his activity are directly political. . . . A poet restricting himself to being a poet without signing petitions or manifestos would immediately be accused of retiring to his ivory tower. . . . (pp. 15-16)

The contemporary artist feels a pressure to make his art

and himself politically relevant because our society has been defined as political. ("A society has no reality for us except in its political institutions, and those institutions take precedence over all others. . . .") The truth of this can be easily noted by reading the daily paper. Five thousand years from now, when men study our age they will have only the vaguest notion of what the day to day lives of people were like if they restrict themselves to reading the newspaper which prints all the news which is fit. It is a political record of America, not a human one. (A history of America should include the reactions of children to the murder of Martin Luther King, as well as the day my four-year-old daughter handed me a drawing she had done of a Vietnamese shooting a soldier.)

Yet, it is difficult to accept completely Ellul's criticism of the committed artist. The committed artist arose in reaction to an elitism of bourgeois artists. The revolutionary movements of the twentieth century are very strict about the role of the artist. In Cuba, the ideal is José Marti, with pencil and paper in one hand and a rifle in the other. It is an image which has caught the imagination of many western youth. On the other hand, perhaps, Ellul is saying that it is more important that Beethoven continued to write the Eroica symphony while Napoleon's army marched beneath his window, that Joyce focused his failing eyes on *Finegan's Wake* and totally ignored the shadow of Hitler falling across Europe. (One finds no references or allusions to the political events of the world in the works of Joyce. Only the life of Dublin.) I wonder, though, what Ellul would do with a figure like Rimbaud, whose poetry has done much to illuminate consciousness, but who spent his life, after his brief career as a poet, as a slaver in Africa. And what about Federico Garcia Lorca who did not sign manifestos or petitions and paid hardly any attention to the Spanish Civil War, saying, "They do not care about poets," and was shot by a Franco firing squad because he was a poet. It was precisely because Thomas Mann was politically involved (or at least aware) and Lorca was not that the former escaped Nazi Germany and the latter died in fascist Spain. Perhaps Ellul is merely questioning the nature of the artist's commitment and saying that signing a manifesto is the wrong kind of commitment.

Another accepted political pronouncement which Ellul considers an illusion is the revolutionary dictum that the revolutionary must take state power.

> The more an individual has become politized, the more he will see and think about all problems as political problems, the more importance will he attach to political action, and consider it the only possible course and, by his attitude, endow that course with a maximum of power and effectiveness. At the same time, the more politized he is, the more will he be focused on and oriented toward that basic political force and form: the state. The more he takes recourse to the state, the more power he gives it. For him the *only* problem is: *who* will control the state? Will it be *his* party? All will then be perfect. Will it be another party? Then things will be bad. But he never thinks of reducing the state *itself* . . . on the contrary. (p. 197)

What Ellul says here is almost heretical. The first step toward a solution is to ignore politics and the state. And, instead of trying to seize state power, "reduce the state."

> The hope must be surrendered that constitutional rules, good institutions or socio-economic changes will modify anything in decisive fashion. The hope must also be abandoned that the citizen will be able to control the state. *Politics is a problem of life*, and of life without respite. The fundamental error in 1789 was to believe that controls over the state could be found in the state, and that the latter could be a self-regulating mechanism. Experience has shown that the state will retreat only when it meets an unsurmountable obstacle. This obstacle can only be man, i.e. citizens organized independently of the state. (p. 202. Italics mine)

"Politics is a problem of life." It is not a problem of economics, or of government, of laws or ideologies.

Politics is a problem of life and only as it is approached as a problem of life is there any possibility of a man having a life. (Abbie Hoffman says, "Politics is what people did with their lives, what they did with their money, how they related to each other.") Ellul leaves unproven his contention that "Experience has shown that the state will retreat only when it meets an unsurmountable obstacle." What experience? What state retreated before what unsurmountable obstacle? Ellul contends that the obstacle is "citizens organized independently of the state." Experience seems to indicate that citizens who attempt to so organize only incur the wrath of the state, because, they are, in effect, rejecting the state. (The People's Park episode in Berkeley is a good example of state reaction to people organizing independently.) The state cannot tolerate or long survive such an act.

But given the lack of clarity in this passage, it is too provocative to be dismissed glibly. Particularly when one looks at the society and sees a black youth culture and a white culture who are trying to separate themselves from the state. In *The Technological Society* and *Commonplaces*, Ellul dismisses the youth cultures and all that they embody as being forces which integrate rebels into society, though their aim be just the opposite.

> Such movements are based on authentic impulses and valid feelings, and do allow a few individuals access to modes of expression which otherwise would have been closed to them. But their essential function is to act as vicarious intermediaries to integrate into the technical society these same impulses and feelings which are possessed by millions of other men. . . . Certain deep ecstatic instincts and impulses would otherwise escape the jurisdiction of the technical society and become a threat to it. (*The Technological Society*, p. 426)

Ellul minimizes the reaction of the dominant society to the youth cultures, a reaction which has become increasingly hostile. Long hair (be it shoulder length on a white male or Afro high on a black male) communicates an attitude of mind and a manner of being which the dominant society regards with extreme hostility. The Marine Corps was facing a full-scale revolt until it issued an edict tolerating the Afro cut. Black bus drivers and policemen have been fired for wearing beards. Hair on the head and face has, in contemporary America, a political content which is not illusory. An antagonism toward any youth not resembling Julie and David Eisenhower exists today which amounts to an undeclared State of war. Ellul fails to recognize that the youth culture has assumed an importance it would not have because people under 25 comprise more than 50% of the population. And it is the youth of a society who will carry that society on. Ellul minimizes the revolution in consciousness which many youth are undergoing, a revolution which constitutes a direct threat to the society. Roszak describes the youth culture as going "beyond ideology to the level of consciousness, seeking to transform our deepest sense of the self, the other, the environment."

Ellul's failure to understand the youth culture is further exemplified in his comments on jazz.

> . . . jazz soothes the Negroes' bitter longing for freedom . . . it is the music of men who are satisfied with the illusion of freedom provoked by its sounds, while the chains of iron wind round them even tighter. (*The Technological Society*, p. 425)

No. Jazz, the Jefferson Airplane, the Beatles, *et al.*, help one establish and maintain a separate identity from that imposed by the society. Jazz, soul music and rock are weapons of survival, not an opiate. John Lennon's statement that the Beatles were more popular than Jesus Christ is more profound than it may appear. Indeed, the Beatles and Bob Dylan and the Jefferson Airplane are the spiritual leaders of a generation.

The youth cultures are more important than Ellul realizes because they repudiate politics. It was the youth culture which had Be-Ins—a mass coming together to do nothing but *be*. No speeches, no marches, no slogans.

Be-Ing. Within the youth culture there has been a return to traditional cultures (Oriental religions, American Indian customs, astrology, folk music, drugs), cultures whose ultimate concern (in the sense which Tillich uses the term) was, in essence, Be-Ing. (This same return to traditional cultures is an exact parallel to what is happening in the black youth culture, which is beginning to study African religions, rhythms, music, to learn what are those things which are uniquely black.) Gary Snyder, one of the fathers of the youth culture, defines that culture, significantly, as 'the tribe.' And it is worth the time and space to quote him extensively on. (The quotes and summary are from Snyder's book *Earth House Hold* New Directions Paperback.)

> We use the term Tribe because it suggests the type of new society now emerging within the industrial nations. . . . In the United States and Europe, the Tribe has evolved gradually over the last fifty years . . . in response to the increasing insanity of the modern nations. As the number of alienated intellectuals, creative types and general social misfits grew, they came to recognize each other by various minute signals. Much of this energy was channeled into Communism in the thirties and early forties. All the anarchists and left-deviationists—and many Trotskyites—were tribesmen at heart. After World War II, another generation looked at Communist rhetoric with a fresh eye and saw that within Communist governments (and states of mind) there are too many of the same things as are wrong with "capitalism"—too much anger and murder.

This led to a rejection of Marxism as being "off the track" and to a study of India and China, early Taoism, The I Ching, yin-yang theories, to Zen and Buddha-Dharma. This in turn led to a realization that there were certain truths in the Eastern philosophies which were independent of the cultures from which they had come. Hinduism and Buddhism, like Christianity, "as social institutions had long been accomplices of the State in burdening and binding people." But once shorn of the institutional and political appurtenances, there existed a

110

truth which after further study was also apparent elsewhere, in "peasant witchcraft in Europe, Tantrism in Bengal, Quakers in England, Tachikawa-ryu in Japan, Ch'an in China." (See Aldous Huxley's *The Perennial Philosophy* for an explication of what Snyder calls "the Great Subculture.")

This Great Subculture, which exists in the East and the West, outside of politics and established religion,

has taught that man's natural being is to be trusted and followed; that we need not look to a model or rule imposed from outside in searching for the center; and that in following the grain, one is being truly "moral." It has recognized that for one to "follow the grain" it is necessary to look exhaustively into the negative and demonic potentials of the Unconscious, and by recognizing these powers—symbolically acting them out—one releases himself from these forces. By this profound exorcism and ritual drama, the Great Subculture destroys the one credible claim of Church and State to a necessary function.

All this is subversive to civilization: for civilization is built on hierarchy and specialization. A ruling class, to survive, must propose a Law: a law to work must have a hook into the social psyche—and the most effective way to achieve this is to make people doubt their natural worth and instincts, especially sexual. To make "human nature" suspect is also to make Nature—the wilderness—the adversary. . . .

We came, therefore . . . to suspect that civilization may be overvalued. . . . Everything we have thought about man's welfare needs to be rethought. The tribe . . . is the newest development in the Great Subculture. . . .

. . . Nationalism, warfare, heavy industry and consumership, are already outdated and useless. The next great step of mankind is to step into the nature of his own mind—the real question is "just what is consciousness?" . . . .

The Revolution has ceased to be an ideological concern. Instead, people are trying it out right now—communism in small communities, new family organization. A million people in America and another million in England and Europe. A vast underground in Russia, which will come out in the open four or five years hence, is now biding. How do they recognize each other? Not always by beards, long hair, bare feet or beads. The signal is a bright and tender look; calmness

111

and gentleness, freshness and ease of manner. Men, women and children—all of whom together hope to follow the timeless path of love and wisdom, in affectionate company with the sky, winds, clouds, trees, waters, animals and grasses—this is the tribe.

Ellul's response to Snyder's point of view is very interesting and deserves to be quoted in full.

If we consider modern peoples in countries where the standard of living is high, do we see the emergence of a culture? Up to now has the United States had a culture that may properly be called original, new, indigenous? Here again, almost everything comes from the outside: people, ideas, forms. And if we consider peoples who have a culture and who acquire a higher standard of living, we can make the same observation as for spiritual life. Cultural creativity declines in proportion as the general standard of living rises; the society then begins to exploit the legacy of previous ages, it devotes itself to antiquity and folklore, and when it does not find enough sap in its own past to maintain the appearance of a culture, it seeks transfusions of new blood, which it draws from barbarians.

Thus Rome, when it had become rich and the standard of living was rising, turned to Virgilian or Ovidian folklore, to Greek culture, or to the Oriental passion, and later would seek new blood from Germanic "culture." Thus our European West since the nineteenth century has turned more and more to the Bohemian, the primitive, the Tahitian, and the Negro, in order to rediscover in foreign music and forms a cultural vitality it has lost. Exoticism is always the fruit of a high standard of living as well as the mark of a cultural sterility. (A Critique of the New Commonplaces, pp. 184-85)

Ellul is guilty here of faulty reasoning. He sets up a causal relationship between affluence and cultural sterility, which is that 2 plus 2 logic. Greek culture came from a slave-owning, affluent aristocracy. The cultures of China and Japan came from the highest economic levels of society, not the lowest. Indeed, what is regarded as culture in the West has always been a concern of the aristocracy. Bach wrote for Dukes and Duchesses, as did Mozart, Beethoven, Haydn and many other classical composers. One could make an argument equally as specious as Ellul's for the decline of culture being related to the decline of the aristocracy.

Not only is Ellul's reasoning inadequate here, but he is too far outside the youth culture to appreciate fully how much it exemplifies the very things he considers desirable. While it is true that European culture in the 19th century began to take its inspiration from outside (Africa), the youth culture of America does not have to go outside. Africa is represented in America. America has drawn repeatedly on black culture for its entertainment and spiritual sustenance, particularly in music, dance, speech idioms and fashion. Rome in the first century and France in the 19th drew on that which was physically remote from it. America not only draws from blacks, it is engaged in a battle to live with them (or without them). This makes for a qualitative difference. The white youth culture, which for so long was imitative of blacks, has now assimilated what it learned, made it a part of themselves and created something which is wholly theirs—rock music. Thus, for the first time, the creation of an indigenous white culture has begun. The youth culture is doing what Ellul says is necessary— "to 're-invent' a situation in which life's true problems are not posed in political terms." Ellul fails to recognize the importance of masses of youth repudiating all that their parents represent. The youth are the future incarnate and the white and black youth cultures are exemplifying a way of life so radically different from that of their parents that, if they continue, the future society they now embody in embryo will be radically different from that which their parents want to bequeath to them.

Parenthetically, it should be mentioned that Ellul is a Christian and any solutions he puts forward are within the Christian framework. It is therefore rather surprising that he nowhere refers to or mentions the mystical tradition in Christianity, for it is this which Gary Snyder is relating to. It is to the thread of mysticism in human experience which the white youth culture from its perspective and the black, through Africa, are returning. And this is totally different from Rome imitating Greece.

If one accepts the new definitions put forth by Ellul in *The Technological Society*, then it is evident that it is exactly this which the white youth culture is reacting to and rejecting. It is also evident that the radical political movement is trying to tree a possum by chasing a coon. When one examines the present radical political movement, with its fratricidal in-fighting, endless and meaningless ideological arguments, it is terrifying to think what would happen if it were to assume State power. The thought of Eldridge Cleaver in the White House and Mark Rudd as Attorney General should not fill hearts with gladness. The *modus operandi* of the radicals differs only from that of the government in the matter of rhetoric. The effect of either is the same—the death of the individual (which has nothing to do with individualism). Both demand that the individual subject himself to it—the revolution, on the one hand; the State on the other. If the ultimate aim of revolution is the liberation of man within himself (and from that all else proceeds), then it is an incontrovertible fact that the revolutionary can bear absolutely no resemblance to the non-revolutionary. The revolutionary must embody and personify the revolution and whenever he demands anything which leads to the subordination of humanity to the organization and politics, he is committing murder. Roszak puts it extremely well:

> Wherever non-human elements—whether revolutionary doctrine or material goods—assume greater importance than human life and well-being, we have the alienation of man from man, and the way is open to the self-righteous use of others as mere objects. In this respect revolutionary terrorism is only the mirror image of capitalist exploitation. As the French students put it in one of their incisive May 1968 slogans: "Une révolution qui demande que l 'on se sacrifice pour elle est une révolution à la papa." ("A revolution that

114

expects you to sacrifice yourself for it is one of daddy's revolutions.") (*The Making of a Counter Culture*, p. 58)

When the radical movement began in 1960, it knew
this. It was concerned with the quality of men's lives and
for the first time since the Abolitionist period, masses
of people were thinking and acting morally. Slowly, and
for reasons too numerous and complex to go into here,
that morality began to be subordinated to politics. The
aim stopped being to change the consciousness of man,
but to raise it to a higher level of political understanding.
People stopped living and started playing roles, stopped
being themselves and played at being Che and Mao.
Now it is a full-fledged five act tragedy, with the revolutionaries holding masks in front of their faces and reading their lines on cue. We are watching a Pirandello play
and mistaking it for the process of Be-Ing.

The critical years in this change in the radical political
movement seem to have been 1966-67. It was in 1966
that the concept of Black Power revealed integration to
be an illusion as the desired end toward which we were
all marching. With it went the black-and-white-together
movement. The first reaction of whites (liberal and
radical) was a mixture of consternation, fear and antagonism. This initial reaction passed quickly for many,
however, and Black Power was accepted (uneasily)
as being for black people. Whites began to turn their
minds to the problem of racism in the white community.
Racism is an attitude. To be defeated, there must be a
change in consciousness, not a change in systems. The
white political movement began to try and grapple with
this.

Stokely Carmichael, who was then the major spokes-
man for blacks, did not have a class analysis of America.
He emphasized race and forced white radicals to give
up any illusions that race could be ignored. It existed;
for too long white radicals had pretended that it didn't
and blacks had acquiesced in the deception. In 1966,
blacks refused to collaborate any longer. There was thus

115

created a tension between black and white radicals. The consciousness of blacks had changed to the extent that they were, at long last, saying what they were thinking. There had to be a corresponding change in the consciousness of whites to understand what blacks were saying. (And a change in the attitude of Be-Ing to live with the new black attitude of Being.)

This tension was good. The old relationship between whites and blacks had been destroyed. The tension was indicative of the beginning of a new relationship. Whether or not this tension would have been creatively productive is impossible to say, because it was short-circuited.

In the winter of 1967, Huey Newton and the Black Panther Party emerged on the West Coast with a ten-point political program and 'the gun.' They viewed the most immediate problem affecting the black community as one of police violence. They would meet that violence with organized self-defense.

While there can be no argument with a man's right to defend himself, there was a sharp difference between the Black Panther Party and the Student Non-Violent Coordinating Committee, the organization of which Stokely Carmichael was chairman. That difference was in aim. Despite the media translation of Carmichael's message, he was explicit, not once, but many times, on his aim: ". . . a society in which the spirit of community and humanistic love prevail." Because he was black, Carmichael limited the creation of that spirit to the black community. If whites wanted a like community, then it was their job to create it. Carmichael was, however, unclear on how this community was to be created. (He has since moved to a political position which is an amalgam of revolutionary violence, cultural nationalism and Pan-Africanism.) However, during 1966-67, the impact of his thinking was to bring about a change in consciousness. (It is in Carmichael that cultural radicals and black studies have their roots.) Most important, there was a moral tone to Carmichael's rhetoric. This moral tone was lacking in the Panthers. The political tone was more in evidence (though the moral tone was supplied later by Eldridge Cleaver, but wedded quite closely with the militant political one).

The Panthers took the concept of Black Power, removed it from its cultural framework, and put it into a political one, which, by 1968, had become Marxist-Leninist. The resultant reaction of white radicals was to turn from working in the white community (which they weren't doing to any great degree anyway) and reenter the black movement via the Black Panther Party. It was a new integrationism, this time under the slogan of Power to the People instead of We Shall Overcome. And once again the illusion of black-white unity was created. The tension which had existed briefly was replaced by an unreal and unequal relationship (the whites being appendages to the Panthers).

Simultaneously, however, the black youth culture and white youth culture were growing and an element of conflict developed between political radicals and cultural radicals. This element of conflict also developed between the Panthers, their supporters and the police. (There were also elements of this same conflict between Carmichael and the government. It is interesting to note, however, that though there was much physical conflict between Martin Luther King and the police, on the broader scale, there was no conflict. Only tension.) Conflict leads to confrontations, and confrontations lead to battles which only serve to increase conflict and more confrontations. With each shoot-out and/or death, the support for the Panthers increased, reaching perhaps its peak with the Chicago slayings of Fred Hampton and Mark Clark. (Ellul is quite cogent in this context: "Any man writing on some wall: 'To the gallows with such and such,' is anti-democratic, no matter what the political crime committed . . . No political action, even if it can be called a crime or be seen as a threat to the structure of democ-

117

racy, no political decision, deserves to be carried to that absolute point of life and death. In that domain everything is relative. It is necessary to help the citizens' political feelings, reactions, and thoughts become less dramatic." *The Political Illusion,* p. 203.) Ultimately, confrontations lead to a resolution of the conflict (the winner being he who is more powerful). The problem, however, may remain unresolved, because the confrontation had to do with resolving the conflict, not the problem which precipitated the conflict.

Tension, however, has an altogether different dynamic, if it can be prevented from becoming conflict. This requires that the two elements try not "to eliminate or absorb" each other. It requires the elements not to get into a state of opposition, for that is the basis for conflict. Tension is a process presupposing the "progression of both factors by a suppression of the conflict which entails the creation of a new tension, situated normally at a higher, more enriched level. . . ." Tension also entails a risk, the ultimate risk. "The risk of a failure or setback is exactly the condition for a responsible human life." (Read the sentence again.) (Conflict also involves the risk of failure, but such a failure means defeat.) The risk of failure in tension "is exactly the condition for a responsible human life." In other words, he who would gain his life must first lose it, must, in fact, put his life in continual jeopardy. Again and again and again. And to move from the individual to the social, Ellul says that tension between social bodies can only "be fertile and serious, if it constitutes [a] true risk for the entire society."

That tension existed for a brief time in the fall of 1966. Black Power personalized the struggle for all who were involved. It was not a matter of pledging allegiance to a political doctrine. It was a matter of gut involvement. The Black Panther Party thrust the tension back into the political arena where it became a matter of doctrine (ideology, philosophy, etc.) and political ten-

118

sion (conflict) was the result. Political tensions "are false tensions, emptying into a void, dealing with nothing serious in the structure of our society, and incapable of producing any solution or basic innovations."

The gut (human) tensions yet exist, but they are either clothed in politics or thought to be unimportant. When all around you are shouting "Power to the People," he who does not feel like shouting likewise feels, of course, that it is he who is wrong, that there must be something wrong with him that he is not shouting with the others. The radical movement makes it even more difficult with its almost daily pronouncements as to who is 'revolutionary' and 'counter-revolutionary.' This is merely a means of intimidating the doubters into subjecting themselves to 'the revolution.' It is a means of saying that it is wrong (counter-revolutionary) to feel human tensions, that revolution is a matter of the head, not the soul. It is also an attempt to create the appearance of unity, us against them, to impose order on chaos. (Chaos is only ordered when the points of tension within it are identified and grasped.) The human tensions must be divested of the political content which has been imposed upon them. ". . . we must . . . leave politics behind, *not* in order to abandon all interest in the *res publica,* i.e. collective and social life, but, on the contrary, in order to achieve it by another route, to come to grips with it again in a different way, on a more real level, and in a decisive contest." How is this done?

> . . . it is important above all never to permit oneself to ask the state to help us. This means that we must try to create positions in which we reject and struggle with the state, *not* in order to modify some element of the regime or force it to make some decision, but, much more fundamentally, in order to permit the emergence of social, political, intellectual, or artistic bodies, associations, interest groups, or economic or Christian groups totally independent of the state, yet capable of opposing it, able to reject its pressures as well as its controls, and even its gifts. These organizations must be completely independent, not only materially but also intellectually

119

and morally, i.e. able to deny that the nation is the supreme value and that the state is the incarnation of the nation. (*The Political Illusion*, p. 222)

A similar idea is, interestingly enough, put forth in Roszak's book. Quoting an Italian writer, Nicola Chiaromonte, he says that dissenters

> must detach themselves, must become resolute "heretics." They must detach themselves quietly, without shouting or riots, indeed in silence and secrecy; not alone but in groups, in real "societies" that will create, as far as possible, a life that is independent and wise. . . . It would be . . . a nonrhetorical form of "total rejection." p. 37.

This sounds good, but, once again, can the state let anyone or any group be "totally independent" of it? For a while, yes, but at a certain point the state is going to have to interfere with those who are ignoring it to insure its own continued existence. It is the dynamic of this conflict which Ellul leaves undefined (which is to say, leaves for us to define).

Political radicals, of course, reject any such idea as being "counter-revolutionary". Perhaps, but Roszak, for one, is not too impressed with what it is to be "revolutionary."

> . . . before we decide that the strategy of "non-politics" cannot possibly work, with its recourse to indirection, involvement by seduction, and subliminal persuasion, let us be honest about one thing. If violence and injustice could be eliminated from our society by heavy intellectual research and ideological analysis, by impassioned oratory and sober street rallies, by the organization of bigger unions or lobbies or third parties or intricate coalitions, by "the flat ephemeral pamphlet and the boring meeting," by barricades or bombs or bullets . . . then we should long since have been living in the New Jerusalem. (p. 154)

Like Ellul, Roszak considers politics to be illusory, an illusion which can only

. . . redesign . . . the turrets and towers of the technocratic citadel. It is the foundations of the edifice that must be sought. And those foundations lie among the ruins of the visionary imagination and the sense of human community. Indeed, this is what Shelley recognized even in the earliest days of the Industrial Revolution, when he proclaimed that in the defense of poetry we must invoke "light and fire from those eternal regions where the owl-winged faculty of calculations dare not ever soar." (p. 55.)

Perhaps the way to reorder a society, eliminate poverty, war, etc., is only through a reordering of consciousness. These social ills which we consider the problems may not be the problems, but merely manifestations of the problems. In other words, these "problems" cannot be solved without addressing one's self (in a continual state of tension) to the spiritual problem underneath. Poverty does not necessarily cease when stomachs are filled. Peace does not necessarily come when the war is over. Freedom does not necessarily exist when oppression ends.

A society implies a definition of a man's potential. Perhaps the way to best realize that aim is to start with a man and not the state. The ultimate responsibility of the individual is to other individuals, not to the state, economic systems or political ideologies. Therefore, it is time to be truly radical and return to the root—the individual—and work from there, but keeping that as the center around which all else must revolve.

This is, of course, doing it the hard way, doing it by "indirection, involvement by seduction, and subliminal persuasion." It is much more appealing to think that the desired end can be attained in one great victorious seizure of power. This is difficult, too, but it is quicker. (And thinking that the quickest is the best is technique at work.) Changing the structure of the state, while quicker, is no assurance that individuals will be changed. There is only one way that that can be guaranteed and that is for individuals to take responsibility for themselves and each other and not expect or ask the state to

121

solve any of our problems. To quote Gary Snyder again: "The Tribe proposes personal responsibilities rather than abstract centralized government, taxes and advertising-agency-plus-Mafia-type international brainwashing corporations."

In The Tribe there is an alternative to what now exists and the political radicals. It is an alternative which begins where others say their actions are going to lead—a human society. The human society can only come into existence if one changes himself and joins with others who are doing the same. Thus was The Tribe created. Thus, the Tribe grows.

Perhaps it is the only hope.

WHITHER ETHICS, JACQUES ELLUL?

STEPHEN ROSE

I can tell you one thing. Jacques Ellul is alive and well in the Committee of Southern Churchmen. But why? Is it because his resolute Barthian No! is congenial to folk who have rightly declared a plague on theological liberalism and its bureaucratic end product, the acculturated American mainline church? No doubt. If Jacques Ellul were running the National Council of Churches there would be no National Council of Churches, because methodologically the way you get Christian unity and mission is a good deal more Christocentric for Ellul than for the sociologically inclined at 475 Riverside Drive in New York City. Chances are that Jacques Ellul would not be given a position of power. He would be a theologian-in-residence, which would be a probable guarantee against being taken seriously. (Both Ellul and *Katallagete* encourage me to speak "foolishly.") Yes, I suppose it is precisely because Ellul is a crack, even pre-eminent, social philosopher, whose sole delight is in Christian apologetics—Barthian apologetics—that *Katallagete* loves him as a brother. For their whole battle over the years has been exactly aimed to prove to the liberal sociologists that Barth's theological science is *truer* (*truer* sociologic-

STEPHEN ROSE is a free-lance theologian, editor-at-large of *Christianity and Crisis,* and founder of *Renewal* magazine. He is the author of *The Grass Roots Church* (1966), *Alarms and Visions* (1968) and *Sermons (Not Preached) at the White House* (1970). He has served on the staff of the World Council of Churches in Geneva.

ally as well as theologically and prophetically) than, let us say, the utterances of those who "began with the world." And since Ellul is a layman (not a tainted cleric) and an authority on ethics, technology, propaganda, law and history, who appears to us, like Bill Stringfellow on these shores, to be uncompromisingly Barthian, one could see how he'd be alive and well in the Committee of Southern Churchmen.

Perhaps it is because no American theologian (save Stringfellow, but we don't really accept the lay theologian, though Barth did) has emerged to press upon all of us the Christocentric alternative. Barth has had no popularizer. Ellul is hardly easy. He seems to have inherited more than a point of view from the Swiss master; his writing, in translation at any rate, is often cumbersome to say the least. But by reaching across the Atlantic *Katallagete*, with this issue, is saying at the very least that no American is telling it like it is. The Death of God theologians are found to be either extra-Biblical or wed to a romantic version of post-liberal radicalism—the new optimism from Prufrock to Ringo, that sort of thing. The partisans of the secular city didn't and don't see the oncoming rise of totalitarianism that seems so clear to Campbell and Holloway. *Ergo* secular city theology is a bit naive. Perhaps there is no such thing as pop Barth.

Then too there is an obvious reason for calling up Jacques Ellul—his radical individualism, his Barthian rendering of the plaintive song:

> *You've got to cross that lonesome valley,*
> *You've got to cross it by yourself.*

More than most, Ellul helps to revive individualism, perhaps more accurately, subjectivity, as a respectable starting-point. Liberate a Barthian respect for the Bible from acculturated fundamentalist roots and you get a pretty free sort of person whose liberty is centered on the Christ event, but whose intellectual range is nuanced by the range of the entire Bible and (because he is free) the

124

whole range of the perceived world. For years we have been told not only that we had to go at life through the Bible, through the Church experience, and not around it. Now the *Katallagete* folks are beyond the institutional church, but they are not beyond the very elements that would be turning the institutional church upside down if it were not for the acculturated conformity that distorts the Good News within the institutional structure.

Two brief autobiographical notes on Ellul:

His sketchy article, "Between Chaos and Paralysis," published in *The Christian Century*, June 5, 1968 had a determinative effect on me. In the article, Ellul tells us essentially that we have reached an impasse in history. We need desperately to find a way between chaos (anarchy, totalitarian repression and inevitable counter-movement) and the paralysis that could ensue if impersonal technological forces in the hands of politicians could indeed dominate our entire existence, removing our autonomy. In my view Ellul emerges as an authentic Christian revolutionary, one who no longer derives his motive power from antipathy to the institutions he opposes, but rather seeks to build the new world in dependence upon some miracle of the Spirit. Here is his basic argument:

The old forms which once nourished man are dying—the church, the family, the community. The new rigid bureaucratic structures are rising to menace what is left of our humanity. There is only one way to deal with the danger, says Ellul. We must start with the individual. But he points out that, despite America's traditional emphasis on individualism, our society "is one of the most destructive of the individual." He elaborates:

> When I speak of the individual, I have in view neither individual religion nor private enterprise, neither classic democracy nor individualistic philosophy. These are all outdated and doomed forms, and it is useless to try to revive them.

125

Ellul continues:

> When I speak of the individual as the source of hope I mean the individual who does not lend himself to society's game, who disputes what we accept as self-evident (for example, the consuming society), who finds an autonomous style of life, who questions even the movement of this society. This individual must make a radical diagnosis of the situation, must live in even renewed tension with the forces of society. But at the same time he must watch himself lest he play a superficial game.
>
> Thus the hippies do not at all have the needed orientation. Strictly speaking, the hippies question nothing, but limit themselves to attempting to destroy forms that are already peripheral and indeed do not exist save insofar as the technico-economic infrastructure of society exists. The hippies can exist only because outside their ranks there is a society that functions, works, administers and so on. They are as it were the human product of that very super-luxuriousness of society that must be resisted.

It is when Ellul seeks to define what the individual must *do* that the going gets even rougher than it has been so far. Basically, the individual pioneer who lives a life in opposition to social structures must stand up against "networks of information, public relations, propaganda" and assert his right to be the judge of what he sees, the decider of what he does.

The individual—each individual—will find it important to reformulate the three areas of existence that Ellul sees as essential: the passions to create, to love, to play. True creativity would constitute a way of acting that cannot be taken over by the society or integrated into "the system." When creativity becomes merely fashion or conformity it loses its meaning.

Love, like creativity, requires new forms. For Ellul sexual laxity constitutes merely a parody of love. And yet something beyond the present structure is needed. For example, Ellul would not want to see the impulse to love "appropriated into the hardened forms of conformed Christianity."

126

Finally, the passion to play: this alone must be the basis for anyone's participation in a group. However serious an enterprise, however important the stakes and the values to be realized, these must not induce us to participate (in political life, for instance). All that . . . is part of the very technical structure that must be opposed! But if, on the contrary, participation is prompted by the passion to play, then it is free; it gives life to the group and at the same time permits the individual to express himself. But note that when I speak of play I mean the opposite of what our society offers us as such—spectacles, novel displays, TV, etc., which debase the passion to play.

Ellul concludes his section on play with a nod toward the festivals held by the so-called primitive peoples.

I think this demonstrates Ellul's perception of the impasse, but beyond his analysis of the crisis, it is his prescription that strikes me as having great truth. Though he rejects conformed Christianity he insists that it is within Christianity that the seeds of the coming revolution lie. I can only say that this is what I think too. To live beyond the present we must have faith in the Resurrection. We are at a point of discontinuity when the intervention of the Spirit is our only hope, when we must cast ourselves on the God of Jesus Christ. Christians (if we only believe!) are capable of "bringing about the great mutation of this civilization."

So a brief article by Ellul clarified for me why I (disillusioned by the church) could not relinquish my insistence that the root of any radicalism I possessed in the social realm was not Marx or Freud or a desire to be in with the New Left or loved by Blacks. The root was this faith, this gospel, this voice calling us into the new world. How can I say it? Negatively, the saddest moment for me in recent months came when I stood on the floor of the National Council of Churches Triennial meeting—which I had been helping to confront with issues related, I thought, to church renewal—when I stood and sought to make a simple proposal. The chairman said that the order of the day required waiting until another time—a

127

time when any consideration would be impossible. (The proposal was that there be some specific commitment to include the voices of the dissenters and dispossessed in future decision-making.) Angered, I said, as I recall, "My order is not the order of this meeting." Arrogant me. Then I said: "I just want to say that I did not come here this week to stand for one side against another side, but to raise questions about the nature of the church." I can't remember the words. My point was that I could live with disagreement between Christians. But I could no longer take the attempt of the churches to pass off theological-ecclesiological issues as social issues, to see everything in narrowly political terms, to refuse to face the evangelical possibility raised by people like Ellul— namely, that any beginning of renewal involves a *real* recognition of the death of our present institutions. The sadness came at the point of my saying something to this effect. It was met by groans and expressions of unbelief. Had I violated Ellul's dictum? Going into the old institution and trying to reform it, rather than staying away and praying for the advent of the new possibility? I don't know. I only know that I meant what I said.

The issue need not be raised so personally: It is the old inside-outside issue. From the perspective of individualism, it is no problem at all. Quite obviously redemption does not depend on where you are, what you believe in the human sense, or on anything that man does. It is the gracious advent of God in Christ lifting up the person who confesses the end of all his devices, the impossibility of redemption in the ethical or aesthetic spheres (Ellul approves of Kierkegaard). But if we move beyond radical individualism (as one suspects neither Kierkegaard or Ellul could do) to the sociological realm, then the Christian is involved in decisions about strategy, and it is obvious from reading Ellul that one could derive sociological strategy from his analysis, even if the sociology is that of the radical individualist. What is needed, I think, is some reworking of the idea of the two realms, so that we recognize in the community of faith the integrity of personal forgiveness before Christ and at the same time the possibility that this individual experience has light of its own (biblical light) to cast upon decision-making. Ellul implies that (sociologically) there is nothing to be done within present institutions. They are all counter-revolutionary or somehow on the wrong track. So we are to live without faith in them, seeking to overthrow them by creating paradigms of the New Order. Presumably his goal would be the autonomous new community restoring love, work and celebration. But here he gives only hints, no guidance.

Which leads us to the question, which is aggravated by a reading of Ellul's sociology—*Propaganda, The Political Illusion, The Technological Society:* Is Ellul underneath it all a perfectionist who sees nothing in the present order that a) is worth praising, or b) he can lead to become the new church? A few summers ago I spoke very warmly of Ellul to two men, one a European with sympathy to the Pentecostal experience, the other a ranking renewalist not yet alienated from the church establishment in the USA. Both men said that Ellul was just a frustrated man who had never been "accepted" and who spent most of his time railing against the fact. He had nothing really constructive to offer. A Barthian perfectionist could sound like Ellul. On the other hand if Barth were writing sociology, would it be different from Ellul's? I think not. It would note the tragic limitations of worldly orders and suggest the more humane possibilities and then move to the inevitable conclusion of practically every Ellul work: Only a miracle of grace can redeem that which is objectively damned. Perhaps Ellul should add the Christian apology to his sociological works, for otherwise they are spirals of down-tending pessimism. His preaching is triumphant. Ellul will find brothers among those who are reluctant to lecture any more, but who are more than happy to *preach*. Or to put it another way: those who could not offer optimism in a lecture, but who *could* in a sermon. Perhaps the Christian *perfectionist* is the man who, having elected the sermon, hesitates to choose a particular text which might, by virtue of its being chosen, provide a particular cultural context for the incarnation of the church. One might argue that Luther's justification by faith is an instance of a particular facet of Biblical truth intersecting (becoming incarnate) with history to kindle a reformation. One does not find a particular thrust in Ellul's preaching —beyond the *No, Non! Nein!*—though one might anticipate one and hope for its emergence in his *Ethics,* a series of many volumes which will, when complete, clarify his preaching.

The introductory volume of Ellul's ethics, titled *To Will and To Do,* has now appeared in English and it provides an example of what one might call the author's perfectionism. On one level the book could be seen as a somewhat tedious account of the paradox that there can be no Christian ethics but that there must be a Christian ethics. This is how the book will be read by those out of sympathy with Barth's (Ellul's) radical sense of discontinuity which leads to the rejection of all natural theology. (Unfortunately, the present volume does not have the appearance of an *introduction,* with more to come, which could add to the impression that Ellul is merely disposing of ethics in order to propose his own, and then not proposing. The volume should be seen as a setting of the stage.) If we give Ellul the respect due him, we will perhaps see that *the establishment of the paradox* is precisely his goal. In which case we must ask whether his purpose is really only to cut off all dialogue, or whether he (and a handful of others) is actually carrying a biblical Barthian light that is (really) obscured in the bulk of what passes for theologizing by today's theologians.

Perhaps the following, from *To Will and To Do* will illustrate the point under discussion:

130

Faced with the necessity of an incarnation of the faith, one feels the need to state Christian truth in such a way that it can be lived. From that moment on we witness a theological effort which ends in heresy.

Ellul goes on to argue that virtually any theological alliance with sociological trend "cannot lead to a new theological education in the truth." But one is tempted, recalling Ellul's own summons to Kierkegaardian subjectivity to ask: Whose truth? Yours, Jacques? Or the truth of Jesus? And (obviously) if the latter, is it never incarnate? Suppose we *know* (with you) that systems atrophy and suspect (as you seem to) that the world is headed not for glorious revolution but for (humanly speaking) disaster. Is there not then a basis for adding to our iconoclastic rejection of any system (and of uncritical affirmation of any *side*) the right (obligation) of the Christian to suggest if not an ethic, at least an occasional denunciation or imperative?

And indeed that is where Ellul leaves us in concluding *To Will and To Do*. We need to develop an ethic *despite the dangers* because "we cannot escape the necessity of responding to these questions: What is the meaning of the fact of being liberated by Jesus Christ from the tyranny of things, and so of regaining the possibility of using them without being enslaved by them? What is the meaning of being committed by Jesus Christ in a true encounter with others, and so of regaining the possibility of serving them and loving them? What is the meaning of the fact of being enlightened by Jesus Christ concerning the destiny of the world, and so of regaining the possibility of serving God and of loving Him with all one's heart, with all one's soul, and with all one's mind?"

In between Ellul's No and his Yes to ethics there lies an extended examination of the limits on various approaches to "morality." If Ellul's final point is well-taken, we may draw at least these conclusions from this and much of his other work:

131

1) It has the effect of stopping us *in this moment* and asking us to refocus our lives *now* on the basis of the revelation of God in Jesus.

2) Assuming that such an approach is seen as naive, dumb or plain inadequate, Ellul is well prepared to demonstrate the inadequacy of alternative systems, both in terms of their inferiority to the Christian revelation and in terms of their demonstrable dangers.

3) Assuming the questioner is still not convinced that Ellul's Christocentric focus is adequate, Ellul tends to invite that person to stop deluding himself that he is functioning as a Christian. That person may be functioning as a natural man and presumably Ellul would not pass judgment on the natural man who thinks "naturally." He would reserve his fire for the Christian who, having the freeing access to the revelation that continually frees and draws man away from closed systems, should not settle for anything less, on pain of losing precisely the cutting edge that the world needs at all times to keep from fatal paralysis or unconstructive chaos.

We must wait the constructive portion of Ellul's ethics to see where he will center down as a Christian thinker. As of now he is the brilliant Christian pre-apologist who is (or has been) reluctant to do much more than clear away the debris of falsely optimistic theological and social thinking with an almost Gaullist disdain. One hazards the guess that the leap of faith for Ellul will be not merely the affirmation of Christ which he has already made but the affirmation of how that Christ is incarnate today—of where Christ's body, the *church* is. We know already that Ellul will not tolerate a church where one is not free, or where the consciousness of dying daily is not present. His theology already depends, and doubtless *will* depend, strongly on the Spirit, the miraculous creation among men of what men cannot create. We've had a hint in *Violence* that Ellul is capable of taking the Biblical witness and turning it into an uncompromising *sermon* . . . in this case against violence. Perhaps we should end up grateful for Ellul the preacher, exonerate him of perfectionism, and simply await the rest of his ethics as a continuing sermon. My verdict at the moment is that Ellul has stated the case for a Biblical Christianity and an ethics of exegesis and exposition. It remains to see whether everything will come together in a culturally (incarnationally) constructive sense. And to *that*, of course, Ellul would rightly contend that only the Spirit can finally say.

THE AMERICAN IMPORTANCE OF JACQUES ELLUL

WILLIAM STRINGFELLOW

If—say, about the end of the decade—there be any
survivors of the death of the American culture, and,
should any of them be theological literates, and, if, while
sifting the rubbish, they happen upon a book or two
by Jacques Ellul, they will surely be mystified as to why
a message so intelligent and urgent was not more heeded.
If attentive to Ellul, a survivor would behold an ethics
of society with redemptive capabilities: an ethics which,
it would seem, would have been welcomed in a nation
beset by disintegration, social and moral, of the scope
that the ruins would evidence.

Perhaps Ellul's word would not, in itself, if not neglected or suppressed, have been sufficient to alter events
—to obviate or forestall the collapse of the American
social order, but at the least it would have edified the
calamity. What Ellul has written, which has been published in America, discerns so much of what has been
essentially and characteristically corrupt in America. His
book *Violence* is an example of that. That violence is
the literal ethic of death does not mean that non-violence
is the way of life, or that non-violence is even non-
violent, and it does not mean that a conscientious man—
a Christian, for instance—may not participate in violence

WILLIAM STRINGFELLOW is a lawyer, writer and theologian
whose books include *A Public and Private Faith* (1962), *My
People is the Enemy* (1964), *Dissenter in a Great Society* (1966),
Count it All Joy (1967) and *A Second Birthday: A Confrontation
with Illness, Pain and Death* (1970).

even while confessing that violence is the ethic of death. How very much the Americans, during the fifties and the sixties needed to understand all that, what with Selma and Saigon and Dallas and Memphis and My Lai and Chicago.

Survivors might suppose that Ellul's work became available to Americans too late to influence them much, but Ellul's writing first became generally accessible in English in 1951, when *The Presence of the Kingdom* was published. That book is the germinal Ellul, and it was timely. In truth it was a prophetic book, yet it was overlooked or dismissed by theologians, not to mention citizens, perchance because Ellul is not an American, and the inference in the aphorism about prophets (that they are honored outside their own countries) is probably unjustified in any case: prophets are unhonored everywhere where their insight applies.

Some of the early Ellul theology published in the United States suffered, it must be mentioned, from inept, undiscerning, even misleading translations from the original French and that, no doubt, was a deterrent in both their circulation and comprehension; still, translation was not a consequential issue with Ellul's later and, significantly, more definitive theological ethics, notably, *To Will and To Do* and *The Meaning of the City*, both of which appeared ten years before the American crisis reached apocalyptic magnitude. Both of these books are devastatingly lucid and perhaps their very clarity and, really, simplicity inhibited American theologians and ethicists from confronting Ellul as theologian and ethicist.

Neither problems of faulty or facile translation, nor the implicitly threatening radicality of Ellul's thought were inhibiting for some other Americans, outside the professional precincts of Christendom, from learning from Ellul and from dealing with his challenge. Back in the early sixties, some lawyers, sensing the moral stagnation and commercial subservience of American legal education and practice, were introduced to Ellul's *The Theological Foundation of Law* in which Ellul, himself a lawyer, exposes natural law, in its multiple versions, as a decorative but decadent facade for stifling human life. While, manifestly, the law in America remained corrupted commercially, for the most part, and became, toward the end of the decade of the sixties, highly political and, in fact, an instrument of totalitarian abuse (for both Green Berets and Black Panthers, as it were), there was a definite impact, attributable to the ideas generated through Ellul, upon the legal profession. There were substantive changes in law school curriculum; there were some lawyers on the scene, in the ghettos, in the political trials, in the thick of the struggle against the totalitarianization of American society. If they were outnumbered, if they can be said to have failed, it was not because of default, not because they were not engaged at the right time in the appropriate places. Ellul, fittingly, given his own involvement in the anti-Nazi resistance and later in the opposition within France to the Algerian war and its atrocities, was an instigation for their efforts.

Much the same can be recalled about Ellul's recognition and inspiration to assorted social and political scientists in America during the years of final crisis. Ellul's studies—*Technological Society, Propaganda,* and *Political Illusion*—had a considerable currency and application in these disciplines which, in a way parallel to what happened to the law, had become pedantic and obtuse and, to a large extent, prostituted to politics and commerce at deadly, literally deadly, expense to human beings and to human life in society. For many social scientists who sensed the revolutionary needs of America, Ellul and these works of his were symbols of the realism and freedom required to refute the Patrick Moynihans, the Arthur Burns, the John Mitchells, and, indeed, the Spiro Agnews.

Perhaps if the moral theologians of the day had re-sponded to Ellul's theological ethics in some way similar to those minorities of lawyers and political scientists and sociologists it would have been catalytic. Perhaps the fragmented and isolated witness of the few in the law and in politics and in the other social disciplines would then, somehow, have found greater coherence. If nothing else the ranks which stood against death in society would have been increased: the few would have been a few more. Maybe even, if the ethicists and theologians had bothered to read Ellul and deal seriously with Ellul's theology of ethics for society, the churches—with their immense wasted and dormant strength—might even have been induced to witness. Who knows?

And, amidst the ruins, who cares? The survivors, if there be any, and if any that be are theologically literate, and if they stumble upon remnants of Ellul's books, or if they find evidences of related works of resistance or of revolution or, otherwise, of redemptive significance, will likely never ask such questions. The remains that they dig up pertaining to the American churches, and to "American theology," and to American social ethics, in the opportune years, just before the terminal event, will prove that all of these neither knew nor cared for the concern for life which Ellul represents, and that all of these, in fact, were fascinated and preoccupied and pos-sessed by the idolatry of death.

Or, to put it all quite succinctly: the deep trouble, theologically, in America is that American theological ethics is unbiblical, pietistic, fadistic. Curiously, the unbiblical ultimate, the most pathological pietism, the final fad is a death wish. I believe that to be the Ameri-can message of Jacques Ellul.

138

ON TRANSCENDING
TECHNIQUE

JAMES W. DOUGLASS

In the modern world, the most dangerous form of determinism is the technological phenomenon. It is not a question of getting rid of it, but, by an act of freedom, of transcending it. How is this to be done? I do not yet know. That is why this book is an appeal to the individual's sense of responsibility. The first step in the quest, the first act of freedom, is to become aware of the necessity.

The Technological Society (p. xxxiii)

A simple concern for survival has forced us to be aware of the necessity of technique. On the front page of yesterday's paper, an article describes the prospect for life in the Northern Hemisphere if the present pollution rate continues:

In 1980—10,000 people will die in one metropolitan area of the United States, which will be inundated by a cloud of pollution.

In 10 to 15 years from now every man, woman and child in the hemisphere will have to wear a breathing helmet to survive outdoors. Streets, for the most part, will be deserted.

Most animals and much plant life will be killed off.

In 20 years, man will be forced to live in domed cities.

JAMES W. DOUGLASS has taught theology at Bellarmine College, the University of Hawaii and in the Program for Non-Violence at Notre Dame. During the Second Vatican Council he was a theological advisor to several British and American bishops on the questions of war and peace. He is the author of *The Non-Violent Cross* (1968), and has contributed to *Commonweal, The Christian Century, The Catholic Worker, Continuum* and other journals, and is completing a book on resistance and contemplation.

139

The technicians' solution? "We can put on a semi-space suit and roam around a deserted and dead country. The people will be inside and all living things outside will be dead. Technology will have taken over completely."

For those who have confronted the threat of nuclear war, the vision is a familiar one: . . . a deserted and dead country . . . the people "inside" . . . men in glass masks roaming a landscape of death. Only in this case, the techniques behind it all will have been more gradual, more peaceful, an inevitable accompaniment of technological progress. The counters on the space suits will measure not radioactivity but pollution. The survivors will be, as after a nuclear war, white, educated, and armed—but dedicated to a crash program for lower-income breathing (awaiting only the recommendations of a Presidential commission). Ethical debates will recall earlier dilemmas: What to do if my "clean air room" is too small to include my neighbors? The churches will pray for air. The Pope, in a slightly more habitable climate, will appear without helmet on his balcony as a sign of hope to the world. The Third Vatican Council will debate the role of the Church in pollution, with the American bishops arguing that technology is not intrinsically evil. (Wasn't technology responsible also for the life-saving helmets visible everywhere in St. Peter's?)

Whether through the means of war, pollution, or propaganda—all aspects of technique—the end of man seems to be following the pattern described by Jacques Ellul. We live in a civilization of means. The specialist chooses the "one best means," the technical means, in every field from education to weapons systems. It is the aggregate of these means that produces technical civilization. The technical milieu, in its rationality and artificiality, absorbs the natural. Thus the convergence on man of a plurality, not of isolated techniques, but of systems or complexes of techniques. The result is an operational totalitarianism destructive to man—in which, however, each individual technician can assert in good faith that his technique left intact man's integrity. What individual technician will have been responsible for the deadly pollution of 1980? Each technician's ends, even the ends of the system, were altogether different. "Everything today seems to happen as though ends disappear, as a result of the magnitude of the very means at our disposal." (*The Technological Society,* p. 430)

I believe that Jacques Ellul is right in his contention that the forces of death were never more apparent in history than they are today. The "powers" referred to by St. Paul are moving the world inexorably toward a global death. To deny that such is the obvious direction of the world is to succumb to idealism. In *The Presence of the Kingdom* Ellul uses modern war, and the technological society which wages it, to show the solidarity of all men in sin. This is not because, regarded as individuals, all men are bad, but because all are "shut up under sin" (Gal. 3:22): You pay your taxes (or buy your products), and you get your war (or air pollution). Technique, as sin, always conceals in itself a finality which cannot be evaded.

Even the most determined efforts of revolutionary Christians to extricate themselves from this process have only committed them to it more deeply. To many of his Christian readers, the scandal of Ellul is not his indictment of society but, in *Violence,* his rejection of violent revolution and all its Christian protagonists, especially its theorists and theologians. Violence is of the order of necessity. Its necessity appeared as a result of man's broken relation with God. Violence is the necessary technique of both those who hold national power and those who wish to ascend to such power. The Christian who is free in Christ must struggle against necessity and violence, even that done in the name of a revolution of the poor (and usually resulting in the poor's greater suffering).

Ellul preaches instead a revolution of awareness and

141

transcendence: the achievement of an acute awareness of technique's necessity and finality in our civilization, and an eventual transcendence of it by an act of freedom. But on the second point Ellul is less clear than he is on the first. The massive analyses of what is essentially the power of sin, in *The Technological Society, Propaganda,* and *The Political Illusion,* are not sufficiently redeemed by a contemporary statement of grace.

Even in *The Presence of the Kingdom,* the presence is not so much defined as it is suggested. Ellul balks at describing anything so definite as a new style of Christian life, at the same time as he states the need for such. From some of his suggestions, though, the outlines of the Christian revolution appear, and one can fill in the flesh by looking at the current face of Christ in men of faith willing to love and to suffer.

I was especially struck by the following statement in *The Presence of the Kingdom,* as providing a perfect theological preamble to the act of draft resistance which has placed hundreds of young Americans in prison cells:

> The will of the world is always a will to death, a will to suicide. We must not accept this suicide, and we must so act that it cannot take place. So we must know what is the actual form of the world's will to suicide in order that we may oppose it, in order that we may know how, and in what direction, we ought to direct our efforts . . .
>
> Our concern should be to place ourselves at the very point where this suicidal desire is most active, in the actual form it adopts, and to see how God's will of preservation can act in this given situation . . .
>
> . . . it is always by placing himself at this point of contact that the Christian can be truly 'present' in the world, and can carry on effective social or political work, by the grace of God. (pp. 28-29)

The price of transcending a civilization of technique is to suffer in one's own person that civilization's will to death. The conclusion of a young man's spiritually-based refusal to kill on behalf of his society, is that that society will seek to kill him spiritually—through the technique of a "correctional institution". What society seeks to correct by the technique of imprisonment is the resister's conscience, or more basically, the power of the Holy Spirit working in him.

Only when the spirit in a man has been adjusted to his society's will to death, and is thereby dead itself, will society accept his "spiritual life". For "spirit" at that point will mean not a revolutionary power to transcend society but simply a technique of mind for the purpose of survival through social self-adjustment. How often has the spiritual life of the Christian in the technological society done nothing more than achieve his "good conscience," without risking any rupture between his conscience and society's will to death? Such techniques of the spiritual life grant autonomy to the world's will to death by submerging spirit in society and repressing its power to transcendence.

Once the revolutionary power of the Spirit has been adjusted to the will to death, it is only a short step for that society's "spiritual leaders" to go on to spiritualize technique itself. The most remarkable aspect of the moon voyage was not America's technological proficiency, which is just as evident in a supermarket, but the efforts of the churches to give it an overwhelming spiritual significance. When President Nixon claimed that the moon landing was the greatest event in history, Billy Graham's mild disclaimer excepted only the Incarnation, Crucifixion, and Resurrection. He would have been saying more about Christ had he excepted the birth of *any* child and the death of *any* man, more than a few of which deaths can be laid directly to the priorities involved in putting a technician on the moon before ministering to the brother on the side of the road. But the euphoria of the American churches in general would have led one to believe that the astronauts' feat represented, after years of protest and frustration at home and abroad, the *self*-resurrection of America by technique. It had been proven that we could do it. Live in peace? No, build a machine to escape our world of death. (Only we hadn't escaped. The machine brought death with it and left it on the surface of the moon.)

If there is a church of Christ living today, it is not to be found in the act of spiritualizing technique or of sanctifying the world's will to death. I believe that the presence of the kingdom is indeed "at the very point where this suicidal desire is most active," yet that it is present in spiritual *resistance* to that will to death—carrying into suffering practice the life of the Spirit. I believe that the suffering of a single draft resister in his cell, or the struggle of Bobby Seale to speak to American injustice through the gag placed in his mouth, exerts a more powerful spiritual force toward the preservation of the world than the witness of a privileged church. This is not to say that the institution of the Church is incapable of transcending technique, of becoming poor and filled with the Spirit. It is to say that the Church cannot truly minister to men's needs until it *has* become poor, and that in the meantime the Spirit will move through other men in resistance to death. The living Church is the Church of the poor, not employing the techniques and controls of its society but suffering them in loving resistance.

The way to transcend technique is through truth, a fully lived truth, not the rational, disembodied fact which our civilization labels as "truth." Truth is the life and love of the resister, a truth made incarnate in response to technique—technique being an abstract instrument of control in which there is no living truth, only man's will to power. Where the living truth of a man meets the technique of the world's will to power and death—which technique in an earlier day was crucifixion—the face of Christ appears, and the kingdom is present. The kingdom is present today not so much in a cathedral as in a cell, and perhaps less in a monastic cell than a prison cell, where Christ's rejection by the world and acceptance by God is complete. There technique is inflicted on

144

a man for minutes, hours, and years from every wall and corner, from every order of the guards. There is no sound which summarizes more succinctly our civilization of means without ends than the jarring clang shut of a cell door, leaving a man inside alone with his truth. Thus is a man of truth "corrected" by his society. But if he resists that correction by continuing to live the truth and resist death, then the Holy Spirit has a home, and the life of mankind is sustained.

If in the modern world the most dangerous form of determinism is the technological phenomenon, man's permanent source of freedom is still, as Ellul also states, the life of the Holy Spirit. Only the living truth of the Holy Spirit is capable of transcending technique and of freeing man. And men run freely in the wind of that Spirit, rejoicing in its song, only when they have offered themselves and their lives to God's will.

THE EDUCATIONAL ILLUSION

JAMES BRANSCOME

*Old men, of whom I am one—psychologists, sociol-
ogists, politicians, journalists, men of letters, all of you who
praise and charm the young—if you had the least sem-
blance of honesty, you would have to shout: "Death to
the young. Throw them all in jail!" For that, in the end,
is exactly what you will do.*

Jacques Ellul, Commonplaces

*. . . . Hardly is the cry of "Fire!" heard before a crowd
of people rush to the spot, nice, cordial, sympathetic,
helpful people, one has a pitcher, another a basin, the
third a squirt, etc., all of them nice, cordial, sympathetic,
helpful people, so eager to help put out the fire.*

*But what says the Fire Chief? The Fire Chief, he says—
yes, generally the Fire Chief is a very pleasant and polite
man; but at a fire he is what one calls coarse-mouthed—
he says, or rather he bawls, "Oh, go to hell with all your
pitchers and squirts." And then, when these well-meaning
people are perhaps offended and require at least to be
treated with respect, what then says the Fire Chief? Yes,
generally the Fire Chief is a very pleasant and polite
man, who knows how to show everyone the respect that
is due him; but at a fire he is rather different—he says,
"Where the deuce is the police force?" And when some
policemen arrive he says to them, "Rid me of these damn*

JAMES BRANSCOME is Director of the Youth Leadership Development Program of the Appalachian Regional Commission. As
a Fellow of the Ford Foundation, he studied contemporary teaching techniques in the United States. He is on the editorial board of
Katallagete.

*people with their pitchers and squirts; and if they won't
yield to fair words, smear them a few over the back, so
that we may be free of them and get down to work".*
Soren Kierkegaard, Attack on Christendom

This article seeks to examine briefly Jacques Ellul's
understanding of education in the technological era.
Formal education as we have it in the United States is
not directly addressed in any of Ellul's works available
in English, but what he says certainly has application to
the educational circumstances in which we find ourselves.

The reason Ellul has not addressed himself directly to
formal education is that he views such an isolated approach as ineffective. For him, education is the primary
propellant used by the technological society to gain mass
acceptance of the means and ends determined by it. Unlike most contemporary American studies of education,
which analyze education on the basis of university or
school and then relate it to the society as a whole, Ellul
looks at education from his analysis of the technological
society. By so doing he does not concentrate his attention
on useless diversionary subjects—alienation, irrelevance,
defense contracts, etc., etc.—which so excite the attention
of educational reformers in the Ivy League and the New
Left. Rather, Ellul devotes himself to an explanation of
how and why the educational institutions will and must
serve one end: to accommodate students to the technological society. Granted, the issues raised by educational critics have led to needed reforms—more black
students and black studies programs, curriculum changes
to more relevant subjects, a reduction in university defense contracts, etc. But the important point is that even
if all the changes we have put on the priority list were
made, education would still exist to adjust students to the
life styles demanded by the technological society. What
Ellul has argued about politics, economics, science and
society is likewise the situation in "education". For

technique as he defines it encloses educational efforts just as surely as it encloses these other human activities. In a word, the educational enterprise *is today defined by its relation to the world of technique.* Education does not "use" technique, but is used by it.

A case in point, for example, is the way that so-called high-risk programs designed to admit more blacks and poor whites to colleges are predicated on one condition: that these students submit to "compensatory" education programs which on the face of them declare that *nothing* is fundamentally wrong with the educational system which created the culture and culture-bound tests acceptable to the technological society. Rather, the very existence and operation of these "compensatory" programs make it quite clear that the "problem" is the persistence of hillbilly or black or peckerwood in the midst of the massive efforts of education to integrate him into the technological society. From Ellul's point of view the celebrated reforms like the open admission program recently announced in the New York university system are only so many Kierkegaardean "pitchers and squirts" when compared to the real threat that education poses to humanity in the new order of the technological society. We may not have ROTC on campuses in a few years, but we can rest assured that the new techniques of a volunteer army will be able to find all the "educated" and dedicated technicians needed from the system of higher education. Obviously, ROTC and conscription were becoming inefficient—the last thing tolerated by the technological society—and the student militants only increased the speed with which these programs were replaced by a more efficient and more acceptable system.

Ellul's understanding of modern education is based on the emergence of two phenomena peculiar to the technological era. One is the notion that all problems today are viewed as *political* problems, capable of solution only by *political* means which are allegedly controlled by the masses—the political illusion. The second

149

phenomenon is the emergence of a totally new set of techniques, collectively called "propaganda" by Ellul, for adjusting large masses to the necessities of the technological society. These two phenomena are inter-related and use education for their persistence and continued refinement. Political problems today arise in the closed universe of images created by propaganda and conveyed by education. Education itself has become almost entirely a matter of politics and techniques. To the degree that education has not, is the degree to which man in this society has not been sufficiently conditioned by propaganda to insist that education must become *entirely* a political matter, and thus a matter of state. To be sure, educational "decisions" are still being made, but like political decisions, they are ephemeral, pseudo-decisions "determined as to give their initiators neither latitude nor choice," says Ellul. (*Political Illusion*, p. 29)

As in politics, it is in the domain of current events ("news") where educational "decisions" are being made; decisions of appearance only. For example: putting students on committees, ousting demonstrators from a building, announcement of a major "breakthrough" in research (which is really non-news because previous technical procedures had already determined the event), re-structuring the *method* (like team-teaching and audiovisual tools) but not the *content* of education, etc., etc. The actual educational decisions—*who* will be taught and *who* will remain the victims of education; *what* will be taught and the reasons for which it will be taught—these decisions have already been made by the necessities of contemporary life defined by educational technicians. Perhaps the best recent example of this was the Ocean Hill-Brownsville incident, where the Ford Foundation and others were attempting to relate the school system to the needs of the communities that it served. While the attempt was defined mainly as an educational matter, the issues raised as a result of the questions over who will teach and what will be taught, plus the intervention of the media that played on citizens' "current events" complex, reduced the matter to a *political* fact that precluded the introduction of any fundamental challenges to the contemporary failures of education. Ellul sums up the resulting impact on man and institutions with the emergence of these phenomena: "The great new facts, such as our increasing technology, our propaganda and psychological techniques, *and the systematization of all institutions*, attack man and democracy simultaneously; they attack man to make him conform and to reduce him to a mere piece in the system; they attack democracy, by substituting a mythical system for one based on reality." (*The Political Illusion*, p. 226. Italics mine) And that is why, in "this technological society, the normal tends to replace the moral. Man is no longer asked to act well, but to act normally . . . the highest virtue demanded of man today is adjustment." Hence, in the technological society, "education" remains a part of "virtue," but "virtue" as defined by technique, not Socrates: "The chief purpose of instruction and education today is to bring along a younger generation which is *adjusted* to this society." (*To Will and To Do*, p. 192. Italics Ellul's)

Without going further into an explanation of Ellul's point of departure for studying education in the technological society, let me give one example of his disregard for much of the effort educational reformists are engaged in presently in the United States. At the center of the discussion of reform has been the question (asked most often by students themselves, interestingly enough) of what is the end that we are trying to accomplish in the educational process. Ellul refers to this in *Commonplaces:* "Ends are infinitely seductive and infinitely fragile soap bubbles that can shift direction at the slightest breeze and burst at the slightest pressure. Ends are incapable of justifying anything because they do not exist: at the most they are intentions, ideologies, programs. But when a man who has such good intentions re-

151

sorts to the means of evil, he finds himself corrupted by the evil he does, and his good intentions become a farce." (p. 303). Defining, and even reaching common agreement on the "end" of education is unimportant and diversionary because it assumes that those engaged in the decision-making—whether they be in the Office of Education, on the Board of Trustees, or in the student government—are actually in control of the processes and content of modern education. As we shall see, for Ellul this is the great educational illusion.

It is important to recognize that for Ellul, education must be broadly defined in the technological society as a complex of various propaganda techniques. Properly speaking, Ellul means propaganda*s* and uses the term cautiously so as to distinguish this complex of techniques from the idea of ruthless fascist lies we usually think of when we think of propaganda. In the broadest sense propaganda to him is education; education as a formal institutionalized process carried out by the public schools and universities is only *one* element of the system that applies educational (and these propaganda) techniques to accommodate persons to the technological society. To the degree that he addresses himself to educational institutions, Ellul is arguing against the myth that they are in a position to oppose the technological society; in fact, his analysis demonstrates that intellectuals and academic institutions are not only the most susceptible group to propaganda, but they are also the one group most ready to utilize any new educational technique as soon as it is developed.

Propaganda is technique, "the totality of methods rationally arrived at and having absolute efficiency in every field of human activity." Because technique has its own ends, it is impossible to adopt a technical means for the accomplishment of a task without accepting the end that technique has determined for itself: to make man a minion of the technological society. Because educational (or human) techniques as Ellul describes them are in-

152

separable from the framework of economic, political, and mechanical techniques of which they are a part, human technique can work only in conjunction with and never overcome the other ones. It is an illusion, therefore, to assume that educational techniques can be used to oppose the technological society. They will either be used to build the technological society or they will be inefficient and, as Ellul repeatedly reminds us, an inefficient technique is no technique at all.

Ellul distinguishes between modern and past propaganda by pointing out that that of the past was essentially agitational, thus visible. Modern propaganda aims at integration, a special phenomenon of the twentieth century and of developed nations. It is the subtle sociological propaganda which encourages conformity. Its emergence is related to the fact that the technological society "needs total adherence to its truths and behavioral patterns. . . . It is a long-term propaganda, a self-reproducing propaganda that seeks to obtain stable behavior, to adapt the individual to his every day life". (*Political Illusion*, p. 75) It provides man with fortifications after it has separated him from small groupings—such as the family—and isolated him individually into mass society. It breaks down his capacity for reflection and critical thought and supplies him with ready-made thought patterns—"commonplaces"—which answer all problems raised by the inhuman nature of technique.

By inundating man—especially the intellectual—with large masses of diverse and unrelated information, propaganda breaks down his resistance to reject what is forced upon him and puts him in a receptive frame of mind to accept the message of the propagandist. It systematically separates his thought from his actions by forcing him to be absorbed in translating the thought of others into action, or by keeping him so busy with imaginary or ephemeral tasks that he does not have time to synchronize his own thought and action. The separation of thought and action—an emerging phenomenon of the techno-

153

logical society—is the most threatening effect of propaganda to emerge in an identifiable way in the decades since World War II. It has given modern man the capacity to rationalize everything without making him feel he has compromised his conscience or values. Perhaps the best examples in America have been the Cold War and Vietnam. (A recurring theme in the first volume of Ellul's ethics, *To Will and To Do*, is the importance of the Biblical emphasis on the unity of man's thought and action.)

The academic contribution—especially sociology and psychology—to the development of propaganda techniques has been significant. In the field of educational psychology, the enthusiastic acceptance of the philosophy of social adjustment of the student to the society is the best example. The result has been the almost complete dominance of secondary education by technique. New school architectural designs which seek to force the student always to be a participant in a group are perhaps the most blatant example of the attempt to produce a "socially adjusted" student. Psychological tests used to measure a child's self-image for the purpose of determining if he is in the right mental frame of mind to learn are another. By changing a child's self-image, the educational technicians now say, they can make him more receptive to learning. The question of whether a method which deliberately changes the way a person looks at himself is totalitarian never arises, for—as Ellul constantly reminds us—the process is "good" if the child's efficiency (making better grades, being more obedient) is improved.

As we are accustomed to thinking of it, propaganda consists of an attempt by the state or some group to gain adherence to its policy. The propaganda which interests Ellul is not geared to orthodoxy, but rather to *orthoproxy*, a term he uses to distinguish former efforts, which merely persuade, from the modern techniques which act upon the subconscious of the individual without his knowledge and motivate him to act to accomplish goals which have been defined for him by the propagandist. A good example is the obsession which modern man has for participation in "political action" without ever questioning *why* he participates or if his actions have any meaning other than that given them by propaganda.

To introduce his description of educational technique in *The Technological Society*, Ellul contrasts the school of an earlier generation—popularly described today as cold, hostile, disciplined—with that of the modern, inviting school created by "progressive education". The intent of progressive education is to make the child "happy", "relaxed", ready for learning and well-adjusted, capable of being a component of the system. Not only is this method a highly sophisticated technique, he argues, it also requires a master technician to supervise the classroom application. It is important to note that this particular use of education is, as Ellul says, "*a governing principle of every modern political system and of technique as a whole*" (italics mine). The state, of course, is the only institution of the society which is able to carry the burden of implementing this principle. This educational technique also has to be used on everyone, for if someone is left out, it would mean that he would be a potential opponent of the society.

Ellul demonstrates the acceptance of this technique by a statement of Mme. Montessori before UNESCO:

> We must awaken the child's social conscience . . . He must know exactly what he must do and what he must not do for the good of humanity. . . . To secure peace practically, we must envision a human education, psycho-pedagogy, which affects not one nation but all men on earth. . . . Education must become a truly human science to guide all men to judge the present situation correctly. (Quoted in *The Technological Society*, p. 346)

Ellul responds: "Mme. Montessori emphasizes the fact that 'it is necessary to free the child from the slavery of school and family' for him to enter the cycle of freedom proper to this technique. However, this freedom consists in a profound and detailed surveillance of the child's activities, a complete shaping of his spiritual life, and a precise regulation of his time with a stop watch; in short, in habituating him to a joyful serfdom. The most important aspect of this technique is the forced orientation toward it. It is a social force directed toward a social end."

Ellul goes on to point out that abstractions such as "the good of man" that the child is to learn are mainly dependent *upon the regime that controls the educational system*—a seemingly incomprehensible notion to the American "liberal". The object is to integrate the child into the society as a functioning, obedient integer. The emphasis is *not* on the child in this philosophy, but upon the *system* of which the child is to be a part. The key word, says Ellul, is *adaptation*. Man is molded by the educational techniques to accept willingly a society that otherwise would be unacceptable for him. Thus: ". . . education will no longer be an unpredictable and exciting adventure in human enlightenment, but an exercise in conformity and an apprenticeship to whatever gadgetry is useful in a technical world." (*The Technological Society*, p. 349)

The new educational techniques—mechanical ones which address the individual as a member of a group and psychological ones which categorize the individual's psyche—are instruments of propaganda in the technological society because they facilitate the adjustment *of* the individual *to* his education. The social sciences, Ellul explains, are especially convenient instruments for the technological society since behavior must be exact and in harmony with the proliferation of techniques used in every area of human activity today. This means that not moral principles, but "precise technological rules, psychological and sociological" are the criteria for human action. "The external act alone has value, and this should be determined for technological motives. This is one of the principal results of the sciences of man which—in spite of their proclamations and declarations—are all and always sciences impregnated with morality aimed at adapting man to the technological world." (*To Will and To Do*, p. 188)

College entrance examinations and other "achievement" and psychological tests exist for this very purpose. Ellul is especially concerned with vocational education and guidance because it seeks "to card-index the individual totally" and represents "a totalitarian takeover of the young". Great care is taken by the technician to select the right individual for the right job and to mold his habits to that of the machine. The increasing emphasis on vocational training in this country is indicative of the ways that education will tighten the channels into which an educated person can be programmed. Indeed: the Vice-President of the United States has already suggested that this nation has too many students in college and that 70 per cent of this nation's jobs do not demand a college education—all as if the sole purpose of college education was to provide *advanced* "job-training". Particularly disturbing is the way that vocational training has come to be viewed as the channel into which so-called disadvantaged students will be placed.

In Appalachia, for instance, which needs more than 200,000 resident college graduates to equal the ratio of college graduates to population in the rest of the nation, primary educational emphasis was placed on *vocational education* in the Appalachian Region Development Act of 1965. To date more than 235 vocational educational facilities or programs have been established in the region. While the federal government cut almost every educational appropriation for the nation in 1969, it increased the funding of these vocational programs 92 per cent in Appalachia. Statistics now indicate that upwards of one million high school graduates will have to migrate out of the region as economic refugees in the next decade. Little thought or concern is given to preserving the culture and rural style of life exemplified in Appalachia.

157

Appalachian youth have a choice of becoming skilled machine laborers, or starving. This is Ellul's "card-indexing" people at its best.

It is no accident that Ellul's most extensive discussion of two of America's most "serious" topics—education and youth—are subjects in themselves in *Commonplaces*, a collection of essays ridiculing the trite phrases of propaganda which chiefly comprise the thought patterns of modern man. In "There Are One Billion Illiterates", Ellul devastates the modern illusion that the "alphabet is the foundation of liberal democracy". If a man cannot read, he cannot be propagandized effectively, and if he cannot be propagandized, he cannot be governed, goes the argument. While Ellul is not arguing for ignorance, he is attempting to point out that education—and the amount of education—determines the extent to which modern man needs (and is able to consume) the propaganda of the technological society. As Ellul would explain the point in *The Technological Society*, technique is by definition artificial and is opposed to what is natural, thus human. Education, comprised as it is today of techniques, cannot perform the task which the Greeks, the medieval universities and even Kant gave it: to make man human. Educational techniques carried to their conclusion can only make man a pawn of the existing technological order. They are categorically opposed to man as a child of God. Thus, the most appalling thing to modern man is to confront someone who does not have an "education". By today's standards, if one is not educated, he is not human. Nations are judged as civilized or uncivilized, developed or underdeveloped, on the basis of the percentage of the population able to read and write. Eastern Kentucky people are often described as "barbaric" in print and on the media because one-fourth of those over twenty-five are functionally illiterate. But, Ellul reminds us, the point is really not whether one can read or write, but *what one reads,* not whether one is educated or uneducated, but *what one is educated for* (and *where*). Similarly, one is considered "motivated" (i.e., can be educated) only if he is motivated in the same direction as the educational establishment, whether Christ's or Caesar's. Young blacks and poor whites who drop out of the system are not considered wise or respectable for doing so, but "unmotivated". They are society's outcasts because they have rebelled against being programmed into the system. As the editor of this journal has repeatedly observed, this sort of thing suggests that the only relevant issue in modern education turns on *freedom from the educational system;* that education in the technological society must be fundamentally a *dis*-adjustment of the student from the system. And this is the very thing an institution in the technological era *cannot perform.*

The other popular commonplace which Ellul takes to task is the belief that our salvation is the young generation or, "the future belongs to the young". Biologically speaking, he questions how it could be otherwise, but his attack is more substantive: by the time the young have made sufficient profit from the experience of serving on old people's committees, projects, and councils, they are no longer young; by the time the young have begun to participate in the national youth policy, they have become the old climbing the ladder to the top of the trade union, radical establishment, whatever. A recent survey conducted among high school students by a White House Conference on Children and Youth indicates what we may expect from the young:

> 4/5's agree with their parents about the necessity of a college education.
>
> 70% of the students feel that "the main function of education is to prepare one for a good job," while slightly more believe their schools are adequately providing this preparation.
>
> An overwhelming 95% think that school administrators should punish those who break the rules or damage property during a demonstration (59% favored probation or suspension—and almost one-fifth of the students would see "agitators" jailed for their acts).

9/10's think American democracy is the best form of government in the world and 2/3 want a tougher anti-communist foreign policy.

Given this, it is no wonder that we have for the first time an administration in Washington prepared to announce formally a . . . National Youth Policy!

Ellul's analysis of the threat posed by the politics and propaganda of the technological society is important for those who would attempt to reform education. For while they administer "pitchers and squirts," the soul of man is being changed. As McLuhan has noted in a review of *Propaganda*, the technological society has itself become a monolithic "teaching machine". That our educational institutions, even (and probably *especially*) those that are "academically excellent", are opponents rather than supporters of this takeover—that is the educational illusion.

THE DIVINE PERSUASION:
AN INTERVIEW ON JACQUES ELLUL

WITH JOHN WILKINSON

Q.: The Center for the Study of Democratic Institutions has the reputation for having done something to help spread and to interpret the work of Jacques Ellul to the American public, especially in connection with his book, *The Technological Society*. That particular work seems to have become a sort of handbook for a certain rather ill-defined spectrum of young radicals . . .

J.W.: Which doesn't include the SDS or the Blacks, who have their own preoccupations. And, incidentally, it is not true that Ellul "doesn't like young people". It's just that into the "generation gap" between the young and the old, Ellul wishes, like Aristotle, to insert the middle term "mature". I get a dozen letters a week from young people . . .

Q.: . . . who presumably are much more interested in Ellul's social criticism than in his theology.

J.W.: I don't believe that radical youth, most of whom are explicitly interested in revolution, could overlook the fact that the "radical theology" of Barth and Ellul is also politically "revolutionary" in the only real meaning I can give to the term.

This theology is bibliocentric and Christocentric, and, in fact, is historically social dynamite. The Gospels have been productive of more revolutionary movements by

JOHN WILKINSON is Senior Fellow, Center for the Study of Democratic Institutions, Santa Barbara, California. He is the translator of Ellul's *The Technological Society*.

far, from the Lollards to the communitarian movements of the present, than the theology of Marx. When I say this, I'm not thinking of the rebellious nationalism of the Zealots, or of J. M. Allegro's claim elaborated with more ingenuity than success that Christianity was an underground cult of psychedelic mushroom eaters. These probably formed a part (along with many other "inspirations", as Ellul would say) of Jesus' personality, since no man is or can be absolutely one thing and no other. I'm thinking of the effect of the Sermon on the Mount on the technologized society, with its forced efficiency and affluence that will probably choke us all. The revolutionary critique of an existing hypocritical, legalistic but fundamentally unjust Establishment of the rich and powerful, is one of the principal motifs of the Gospels. Lately it has been fashionable to say that Barthianism, however strong the stand it took against the Nazis, is a "closed system" and cannot cope with the evils of today's society. But Barthianism, in its Ellulian form, appears in a totally different light ever since we found that our orthodox ideologies, both Communist and Christian, are presiding over the technological destruction of the whole planet. The "Constantinian era", to use a phrase of Barth, that combined so intimately Church and State, is just ending. It began with making Christianity the State religion and established the long reign of terror of Throne and Altar. Ellul points out, for example, that the traditional early Christian practice of pacifism was, in this epoch, made a heresy in the year 316 by the Synod of Arles. The sublime principle involved on both sides was simply: If you can't lick 'em, join 'em. *Now* what are we to do? "Revolution", in the current use of the word, seems to mean agitating for some vague ideology (with unforeseeable and generally disastrous results) against a social situation felt as intolerable. "Revolution" in the Christian sense, as it was used until the English bourgeois Revolution of 1640 to 1688, meant Christian "conversion" (insofar as it did not refer to astronomy)

162

that has little to do with self-serving and highly particu-
larized interpretations of the Gospel of the kind that
resulted in the rise of Capitalism. Is not such conversion
still the most revolutionary act a man might perform?
Think what a meditation on Dives and Lazarus would
do to the society of power blocs, exploding cultural in-
dices and gadgetry. Ellul himself is a "convert" from
what he calls "no particularly Christian milieu".

Q.: What do his fellow-countrymen in France think of
Ellul?
J.W.: He is well-known, but his books have had far
less influence than in the United States. Hardly anyone
took note of *La Technique* when it appeared in 1954. I
couldn't find any reviews except one in the London
Times.

Because French intellectuals have not read much of
Ellul, it by no means follows that they are unacquainted
with the man. He is in fact not only well-known but
notorious perhaps because of his involvements in the
Résistance and in the worldwide ecumenical movement;
and because French intellectuals all know and have
strong opinions of one another, it may be in the way
that Don Quixote loved Dulcinea, whom he had never
seen, by hearsay.

The economist-philosopher Jean Fourastié, who was
and is known for his sunny writings, has recently acknowledged that technological reasoning and scientific
rationality are approaching the end of their tethers. He
even thinks that "religion", seemingly some nondescript
sort of thing, will regain importance. Fourastié used to
write of Ellul's *rage froide,* but in his recantation Ellul's
name does not appear. The phrase "technological society"
in France (and much more so in America) has become
standard. At first an ascription of it was made to Ellul.
Now, it is used everywhere by people who never heard
of him, and, of course, without ascription.

Q.: Well, it's always something to introduce a word

163

or phrase into a language. The first go-around in any education is hearing a vocabulary.

J.W.: The French Marxist philosopher, Roger Garaudy, said, when he last visited the Center, that Frenchmen and Germans do not think as "linearly" as the Americans who are accustomed to giving "pragmatic" answers to very specific problems. Apart from questioning the general validity of such a procedure, Garaudy said that he had started with Barth (and the *Cercle Evangélique*) and had come to Marxism from the Gospels, without losing his interest in Christianity. Ellul, he said, had started with Marx and come to Barth and the Gospels without losing his interest in Marx, at least as a way of "looking at things". That, he said, gave them much more in common than they could have had in America, where each would have been required to do public penance for his first thoughts before he could espouse his second. Garaudy has been one of the foremost protagonists of the dialogue between neo-Marxists and neo-Christians (that had such important results in Czechoslovakia) of a sort "impossible in the United States that has few Christians and no Marxists". Garaudy, I may say, is a member of the Center's International Dialogue Committee.

Bertrand de Jouvenel of the Sorbonne, an Associate Fellow of our Center, half seriously accused me, on his most recent visit to Santa Barbara, of having completely rewritten Ellul's *Technological Society*. He could see no other way in which "a French Rightist could become the darling of American Leftists". Of course, I had taken no such liberties with Ellul's text. What, I think, de Jouvenel was testifying to, whether he knew it or not, was the powerfully corrosive action on established regimes of an updated version of Christ's social ethic. Incidentally, Ellul himself thinks that dichotomies like Right-Left, and *all* the others so profusely thrown up by philosophers, are paradoxes totally dissolved by the *tertium quid* of God's revelation in Christ.

164

Q.: Maybe the Christian is really revolutionary in this way. The question we put to you meant to ask also whether our radical students are not interested in Ellul's social criticism but *not* in his theology, and, if that be the case, whether this stems from ignorance of Ellul's theology or from the sceptical spirit of the times.

J.W.: I can't completely agree with your assessment of the apportionment of peoples' interest in or knowledge of Ellul's books, except with the stipulation that Ellul has not yet worked out his theology as thoroughly as he has elaborated his social criticism. For example, his account of "faith" or of "reconciliation", in my opinion, to the degree that I can decipher them, leave more questions unanswered than otherwise. For given readers, of course, the center of gravity of interest will fall in differing places. One may fall heavily to the side of sociology, and another equally heavily towards religion, with a third in between. *Prophete rechts, Prophete links, das Weltkind in der Mitten.* Forgive my statistical bent, but I have looked up the number of students enrolled in sociology classes in American universities and colleges, and also the number of those enrolled in courses in so-called "religious studies." These numbers are approximately equal. What the overlap is I unfortunately cannot say but I think it is large. That's a rather gross analysis that doesn't necessarily refer to Ellul. It's clear, however, that some who reject the technological imperative described in *The Technological Society* do not accept Ellul's own grounding of this rejection in theology, much less in Christianity. Many are put off by their reading of this "imperative" as a determinism, as a kind of revival of one of the most disagreeable aspects of Calvinism. But Ellul's imperative is only a determinism because almost no one *wills* to do anything about it, or to resist it. You don't think, I hope, that the American people, with respect to "ecology" are ready to put their money where their mouth is? Alain Clément, writing recently in *Le Monde,* even thinks that most of them actually love to

165

see the environment wrecked and polluted. I suspected this before I read Clément from reading H. L. Mencken and onwards. If the old refrain is true that Ellul is a determinist, the fault is not his, not at all. The interesting thing is that many of the young who accept Ellul's sociology and reject his particular theology are nevertheless interested in the total ontological framework in which his (or another's) social critique is embedded. All phenomena supervene on *some* ground, theologically, philosophically or temporally prior; and we have the duty to illuminate this ground *if* we would escape senselessness. To paraphrase Kant, Ellul's theology without his sociology would be empty, and his sociology without his theology would be blind. These are important things to bear in mind at a time when the universal cry is for "relevance". Students, in my experience, almost always wish to know what system of things or of thought any "discipline" refers to. It's *not* true that "relevance" is a term used without meaning by the young. When over- and highly-specialized teachers prove not to be in a position to say just what relevance their subject actually has, they can be expected to find it agreeable to assert that the demand has no meaning.

Q.: It is often said that the social sciences are "value-free," and must be so in order to be unprejudiced.

J.W.: A "value-free" sociology is a sedulous ape trying to apply positivistic methods that are successful elsewhere but that unfortunately can't be applied here. Its results are totally unstable and subject to change without notice. Since most "value-free" social critics either cannot (or dare not) reveal the metaphysical grounds of their science, they continue to deserve Poincaré's jibe that they have the "science" with the most methods and the fewest results. Anyhow, that whole direction of social thought is dead, or, better, in *statu moriundi*, since some of its practitioners are still walking around. Naturally, there are exceptions like David Riesman or Philip Rieff. Even "logical positivism" has had to introduce meta-logic, or meta-mathematics, in order to speak without contradiction about "positive" sciences like physics; and here many, if not all, of the traditional metaphysical problems arise. I have always noted that the modern strife about the foundations of mathematics completely recapitulates the older strife about the mode of being of universals. These problems require to be answered whether one does it in Ellul's way or some other. (Ellul and Barth, for example, have been usually said to be "nominalists".) We have to give plausible answers to insistent questions, *if* we take seriously any theory of argumentation and persuasion. And one of these problems is that of God. As many European neo-Marxists say: God is not *quite* dead.

Q.: But, cannot "unbelievers" discover phenomena of man's real nature? Barth and Ellul think that such investigators can and do.

J.W:. Yes, these anthropologists can and do. Unfortunately, without being grounded, these phenomena remain *mere* phenomena. They do not, except accidentally, touch the true or the good. For Ellul that can be done only by grounding these phenomena in God's Revelation to man in Jesus Christ. That's admittedly a stumbling block to many; it is nevertheless the position of Barth and Ellul, and it *must* be tested further, and more convincingly than it has been tested heretofore. Both of these men have developed an elaborate dialectic with a view to rendering the traditional answer of "faith" acceptable to a sceptical generation. What interests me is that I think they succeed. You know, a simple kind of Christian piety no longer provides an adequate approach to most people. You are talking today to better educated, or, at least, more sophisticated men, who will not bother to refute you if your urge on them a simple, and simple-minded, piety or faith. They'll just leave you alone to converse with yourself, and the strongest faith will probably not long withstand that treatment. Even most out-and-out paranoids need some intelligent hearing; and if a psychiatrist can't find a way to achieve this *rapport* he can't do anything for his patient.

Q.: We will hear more of Ellul's dialectical theology. But, before going into that, we would like to know something of the circumstances that led the Center for the Study of Democratic Institutions to study Ellul. What event or events led to this preoccupation?

J.W.: Aldous Huxley, who had such extreme corneal scarring (more likely due to faulty surgery than the diagnosed *keratitis punctata*) that one might have thought he could read little or nothing, seemed in fact to have read everything. One day in 1959 he suggested to me that he had just finished a "marvelous book" by one Jacques Ellul called *La Technique*, "a most unrevealing title". According to Huxley, the book had "really made the case" that he had tried to make in *Brave New World*, that he was "jealous of the author's penetration", and further, that the book would become one of the 20th century's most authentic documents of social criticism against that fake liberalism that had fastened onto the world the totally technocratic society and its age of total wars. Huxley repeatedly compared Ellul's work with Spengler's *magnum opus*, and in another way, with the work of Bernanos whom he had been recently reading. If one reads Bernanos' recently published posthumous diatribes against the "businessman's society" and the rejection of Christianity by these men of affairs and their servile Christian prelates, one sees how perceptive Huxley was.

Huxley was the first Regents' Professor at a new campus of the University of California, where I was an instructor in philosophy. On that campus Huxley found only a few colleagues with whom he could talk at all, and together we organized a "study group" that had to meet off the campus throughout the year to discuss Ellul's book. A little serendipity will go a long way even in the most unfavorable circumstances. Up to that time Ellul had been known to me only as the author of some short pieces in

168

the French Protestant review *Réforme*, and of a fearsome diatribe (*The Theological Foundation of Law*) against legalistic Roman Catholic "natural law" based on an obviously Barthian inspired rejection of the Aristotelian *analogia entis*. We could scarcely appreciate, at the beginning, the depth of Ellul's religious convictions, a lacuna that was gradually cleared up to a certain degree during the year by corresponding with Ellul himself, and, later, by his extended theological writings. I would like to add that Huxley had himself been seeking for years a "theology" in the form of Vedantism. Some varieties of that religion bear astounding similarities to Christianity. But there was never any divine person, like Jesus Christ, to act as a *tertium quid* between the material and spiritual worlds. And so Huxley had given up the search for a real bridge between the two. That, I think, was the great tragedy of his life. He wanted desperately to believe but could not. Neither his own rationalistic upbringing, nor the nature of Vedanta itself, allowed him to see how the bridge could be constructed. He quite clearly envied the faith of Ellul and Barth.

Q.: But how did the Center get into the act?

J.W.: Huxley had close ties with the Center, at least after it had moved in 1960 to Santa Barbara. He gave the same assessment of the book to its President, Robert M. Hutchins, who read the French version with considerable thoroughness. It is my impression that Hutchins accepted then, and accepts now, Ellul's analysis of the highly autonomous and technologized social order. But, there was a deeper reason for the Center's interest in the book. The Center, in the pursuit of all its manifold projects and studies, always found the way to any reasonable solution barred by a wall of technology. I believe that it was the late Scott Buchanan who was most troubled in spirit by this impasse. He had sought help from the work of people like Lewis Mumford, but had always been repelled by the "happy ending," like forming a study committee, or setting up an institute. Like Barth and

169

Ellul, Buchanan was put off by all "cheap" solutions. In fact, one characteristic of all three of these men was the refusal of the *billig*. And cheap solutions to the problems posed by technology, religion, and almost everything else, were the style of 1960. The Democrats got themselves elected with the promise of a farrago of cheap solutions. The worst thing is that they actually believed in the efficacy of this grab bag of brummagem quick fixes. That's why they spoke so powerfully to some of the youth.

Q.: Doesn't Mumford, for example, seem a lot less happy today than he used to be with respect to the effect of technology on civilization?

J.W.: Oh, yes. And, so does almost everyone else. It has even become the fashion to be pessimistic about all the ways technology is about to "do in" our culture, and maybe us, too. I'm not sure . . . Well, in fact, I'm *certain* that the present wave of indignation about the environment is just another one of these cheap solutions. It blew up awfully rapidly, like a squall of wind, and will probably die down with equal speed, like most American social criticism, *mea culpa, mea maxima culpa* and then everything is taken care of. It belongs, I think, in the study program of the Smithsonian Institution's "Center for the Study of Short-Lived Phenomena." Our intellectual life consists of a series of seven-day-wonders, like "Dialogue," "Death of God," "Tax Reform," and then on to something more exciting. Just think of all those legislators, politicians and corporate managers, who have latched onto the "ecological" issue with an unending series of bills, policies, and blurbs about improving the "quality of life." In some colleges the Home Economics and the Physical Education departments want to get "ecology" into their titles. It is clear, at least to me, that few of these people have any will or ability to change *themselves*, that is, to undergo conversion along with their titles. I'm particularly amused to see that most of the radiant souls who wrote so scathingly about Ellul's

170

"technological determinism" in the numerous reviews of *The Technological Society*, after its appearance in English in 1964, are now singing the blues about technology, population explosions, environmental crises . . . the whole bag. Now we must even suffer through something called "theoecology." But then, that whole crew of cheapjack, would-be avant-gardists never were to be taken seriously, and never will be. I must confess that I have an extremely imperfect sympathy with the professional, ideological wailers, too, the ones who clasped Ellul to their sooty bosoms in their articles. I never had any strong conviction that any of either group ever read Ellul's book carefully, or even at all. They seem to content themselves mostly by reading each other's reviews. But that's no new thing in the world of letters.

Q.: Did the Center do anything further? I mean, more than read the book?

J.W.: Oh, yes. After each chapter was translated, there was an extended dialogue using the translation as a document. That's the Center's mode of procedure. And we held two international symposia that centered about the Ellulian theses. I had to write, after the second one, that Ellul's book had acted more like an infectious disease than as a serious social critique. The participants, although it had been suggested that Ellul's book furnish a *terminus a quo* rather than as a *terminus ad quem*, simply couldn't get beyond it. Something like the hypnotic power of the fabled basalisk.

Q.: What was the reaction of the Center Fellows?

J.W.: There was, besides much sympathy, much opposition at first. You can imagine that, in principle, a Center for the Study of Democratic Institutions would not take too kindly to Ellul's notion that political institutions, like most other social phenomena, when they are made the object of critical scrutiny, prove to be mere manipulative propaganda devices, however highflown the rhetoric,

171

designed themselves as techniques to make out of some otherwise uninterpreted ideology a course of action in the service of naked considerations of money or power. Such institutions enable you to have the game as well as the name. I cannot say that some of our professional optimists are even now convinced of the value of Ellul's arguments. But, some others of us long ago decided that we wouldn't even talk with those incorrigibles who persist in seeing a rosy-fingered dawn at the end of the technological tunnel. You don't, of course, have to be beastly to these well-meaners. The situation is something like that of the Patent Office who, without being boorish, won't even consider a patent for a device that comes down to a proposal for constructing some sort of perpetual motion machine of the first or second order.

Q.: You have spoken of those who in their reviews were *pro* and those who were *contra* Ellul. Outside the Center, are there many really serious thinkers who have taken sides?

J.W.: Oh, yes. And most of them, if we exclude "mission oriented" social analysts who have "missions" and "funding" from the Pentagon or I.B.M. . . . Well, I think, particularly in the last few years, that most serious thinkers are Ellulians, even if they came on their own to similar results from just looking at the obvious state of the world today, and perhaps never read Ellul or even heard of him.

Q.: For example?

J.W.: Well, there is Herbert Marcuse. He published, long after Ellul, and, I think without ever having read anything of him, his *One Dimensional Man*. There is a startling overlap in these two analyses of the post-industrial social phenomenon. It is hardly necessary to postulate any connection between these thinkers. Marcuse was a doctoral student of Heidegger, who long ago

172

spoke of a "planetary technology." Marcuse, after having done Hegelian dialectics with Heidegger, went on to Marx and Freud, and, as far as I can say, ultimately came up with a synthesis (perhaps that's too strong a word) of a lifetime of pondering. Heidegger himself shows curious reticences about God, or the gods. And his primary text is Parmenides and Plato, rather than the Bible. The metaphysical grounding of persuasive social analysis can be plausible from more than one point of view.

Q.: But, is there not a crucially important difference here? Marcuse certainly doesn't ground his analysis of technology in a God, let alone the *Deus absconditus* of the Barthians. That should make an important difference to you.

J.W.: Yes and no. As far as the "no" is concerned, we can and must take certain social phenomena seriously, whether they have a metaphysical or theological basis or not. The bibliocentric view of the world is not complete, for while the Bible, according to Ellul, is, or rather implies, sociological *facta*, it doesn't by any means imply everything, only those exceedingly important things that God has revealed to us. For the rest, we are on our own. That's the reason Ellul frequently cites the perceptive works of Reinhold Niebuhr. I agree with my colleague at the Center, John Cogley, who says that Niebuhr is not a theologian at all, but an acute political journalist who "uses a theological idiom." For those things that are *not* revealed, or not remotely implied by revelation, an anti-Barthian like Niebuhr can give as adequate a testimony as anyone else; and that's the way Ellul always uses him. And the same must be said for Marcuse, who uses a Marxist idiom rather than a theological. One might point out, however, that the mere elaboration of an "idiom" is probably a long way on the road to a metaphysics.

Q.: Wouldn't Horkheimer and his disciples, like Adorno, of the Frankfurt School be more to the point here?

173

J.W.: Horkheimer's social critique is admirable. In a way it's very much like Ellul's. It issues in the prediction of "the totally administered and totally enslaved world" and, more important, Horkheimer makes of the reproaches of his neo-Positivist colleagues (the "telephone-pole counters") that he pursues "social theology," a virtue. He advocates a return to a theological basis for sociology, not indeed a Christian theology, but something like a hypermodern Jewish one. God is postulated, in this theology as in Barth's, as the "totally other." But, Barth and Ellul have a *tertium quid* that Horkheimer lacks in Jesus Christ, who for Christians is both Man and God. Without such a *tertium quid* Horkheimer's "theology" is like Sartre's "atheism". Barth and Ellul use terms to describe the necessary mediation between man and God that would remind a physical chemist of a "catalyst". Lacking this mediator, Horkheimer's analysis comes to be a theology of "longing" *("Sehnsucht")*. I don't know that longing for anything *in itself* is very likely to produce it. It seldom does for *me*. But, Horkheimer is on the right track; at least, I imagine that Ellul would think so. But, an intractable dichotomy between theory and practice has characterized this school.

Q.: Leaving to one side for the moment the so-called "theology of Hope" . . .

J.W.: . . . which also doesn't necessarily or even usually ground whatever it is *I* hope for . . .

Q.: . . . isn't the Barthian and Ellulian "faith" as little able to produce dialectical conviction as "longing" or "hoping"? Some reviewers of Ellul's theological works see in Ellul's works the old "Protestant justification by faith with a vengeance". And, I needn't remind you that they don't mean by the use of this phrase anything very complimentary.

J.W.: Yes, I noticed that particular complaint chiefly in the reviews originating one way or another in the Union Theological Seminary.

174

I admit that I don't know much about Union except that they are anti-Barthian relativists, always concerned with the *dernier cri* in religion and the cheap "quick fix." I wonder they don't become Unitarians right off and sing hymns to race relations and sewage disposal. Such hymnology is, or would be, gratifying, if it were based on something better than the Cold War. That's not putting it too crudely; both Arthur Schlesinger, Jr., and George ("Policy of Containment") Kennan have burbled —they always speak in the burbling vein—words to the effect that Niebuhr was their "spiritual godfather." Sort of like a bunch of religious Sidney Hooks, trying to forget their pasts and "get with it". Barth, you remember, wouldn't disavow social democracy. That fixed him but good with all the updated Fundamentalists in the United States as well as with the religious liberals, the most profoundly un-Christian types I ever met. But more seriously, I think that a case must be made for the primacy of Christian *faith*. And, if Ellul can't do it, he will be just another neo-Positivist social phenomenologist with a few Christian flourishes. I would still think in that case that Ellul describes the phenomena of our world as it really is, but the deeper meaning that might make sense of his phenomenology, to which I think I referred before, would be lacking. That would disconcert *me* immensely, as if anyone cared for that.

Q.: Hasn't the doctrine of the primacy of "faith" over against "works" become a little *passé*? The Calvinist doctrine *sola fide* has taken a dreadful beating from intellectuals for some time now. How do you propose to rehabilitate it? Or, I should ask: How would you have Ellul rehabilitate it? Can anyone say anything very new after all these centuries?

J.W.: I think that the arguments for the primacy of faith are present nuclearly in the writings of both Barth and Ellul. The centuries-long dispute to which you refer I would be glad to inter and to make a fresh start.

Naturally, the doctrine has been used to justify the worst crimes and enormities, and one would like to avoid any imputation of any of *that*. But even in the crimes of industrialism, the close *connection* between technology and "Christian" faith has been clear, even though the one reinforced the other, quite in the spirit of the Constantinian Era, instead of radically opposing it.

Q.: But, to come back to the preeminence of "faith"...

J.W.: I cannot indicate my thought *in extenso* here. It would take a book. Let me say first that the Center has devoted much attention to the theory of argumentation, that is, to "The New Rhetoric," originally based on the work of that name of the Belgian philosopher, Ch. Perelman. This new rhetoric really represents the revival of the classical tradition that effectively lapsed with Quintilian, which the Greeks, and later the Romans, used as the chief vehicle of rational (and oftentimes irrational) persuasion in politics, law, and "culture". The leading conception of the more or less formal study of rhetoric, in the *good* sense, is that the *rhetor* secure the adhesion of his audience by means of persuasion. The audience, in the best case, would be the so-called "universal audience," and the argument one that "would persuade the gods themselves."

Now, the word in the Gospels translated by "faith" is the Greek *pistis*. It is derived from the verb to "persuade" *(peithein)*. In fact, the verb itself is sometimes used. Whatever St. Paul might have seemed to the Jews or to later generations, to the Greeks, I think, he must have seemed a typical Sophist, again using the word in the good sense. He is even represented in this way in the Bible, at least in the passage in which he is seen preaching in a building in which the regular Sophists gave instruction. It is my contention that the New Testament almost always uses "faith" in this context of rhetorical persuasion. (A. N. Whitehead and Charles Hartshorne have spoken of a "divine persuasion" but in a non-

Bible sense.) It is *never* spoken of as representing some ungrounded absolute, except in bad translations. And, I hold, the passages where "faith" is opposed to "works" also mostly refer to something very closely connected with the act of persuasion.

Q.: What do you think Ellul or Barth would think of such a speculative "faith"?

J.W.: Not much, particularly if some new version of liberal idealism were meant. But then, the faith I speak of here is not speculative at all; it is an immediate with no intervening syllogisms. And, if there is any moment in Ellul or Barth that commands attention it is the dialectical one. Both these theologians display a restless need to communicate with their audience and to receive from it a dialectical "feedback". So much so that Ellul (in an obituary on Jean Bosc) represents his own faith as *tragique et révolté*, in comparison with Bosc's tranquil acceptance of the message of the Gospel. And this, says Ellul, is marked to the extent that he cannot form a "closed system." *Si non rogas intellego.*

You know, a teacher *must* take all allegations of fact or theory, that run counter to his own, seriously. He just cannot accept the "cheap" solution to start with that some part of his *kerygma* is a mystery. He *must* reply, and that as clearly as possible. Ellul in innumerable *loci* insists on clarity.

Q.: Could you give us an example to make your position clearer? For example, if the Trinity *is* a mystery, how can you explain it?

J.W.: I've actually had the experience of trying to clarify the doctrine of the Trinity, in courses in the philosophy of religion, and I couldn't act like Anthony of Padua whose sermons so enchanted the fishes. A student will say, when he is asked to clarify his belief in that mystery: It's a mystery. You ask: Just *what* is a mystery? Obviously, he cannot repeat: It's a mystery. If he has any philosophical insight at all, he will see

177

that he may not say that a mystery is mysterious. He must tell you clearly what is mysterious, at least in a clear verbal proposition. Otherwise, he pretends faith in what is literally "hocus-pocus" or "abracadabra," that is to say, magic. To seize on some cloudy formula, say, "The divine gliggl glops," and to profess faith in it, is not to be a believer but a fool. I must know clearly what I am giving assent to, or I am betrayed into the famous "infinite regress." The Ellulian dialectic always runs in this way. Of course, most self-styled Christians *do* repeat, say, the Nicene Creed, in the foolish way I have described. One part, and perhaps the most important, of theology, is to secure a certain clarity and distinctness that makes a creed or a dogmatic proposition relevant to *something* and, therefore, defined. That is what I interpret the Gospels and the Epistles to be doing, especially that to the Romans but, above all, that to the Hebrews. The language of faith in the New Testament is *always* that of assent, and particularly of degrees of assent, to clearly put propositions. This sort of procedure, so familiar to the Greeks, is the basis of *Christian* faith, in my view. The Old Testament seldom speaks of faith, but of "holding fast" or a word like that.

Q.: But, this only puts the difficulty elsewhere; for a person may sometimes be led, even though he possesses the highest philosophical acumen, to assent to what is false. If faith is not somehow a guarantee of itself, how is it known to be *true*? Do not most philosophers, and many theologians of the present, hold, after they have clarified the meanings involved, that the Christian Message (or parts of it) is just plain false?

J.W.: Certainly. And every believer of sense is subjected to continuous doubt; and that as often as another person, not recognizably an idiot, or even something as relatively impersonal as a social crisis, puts a question to him. I take this, incidentally, to overlap with what Horkheimer, in *Neues Forum*, has called a "theology of doubt", where "doubt" is the tool of "longing".

178

Q.: And, when these crises of doubt arise, how does one get from the speculative, or as you call it, "dialectical" to the real or true?

J.W.: I think that the answer to that must lie in a new version of the so-called "ontological" argument, *fides quaerens intellectum*. Philosophers, even when they rejected it, as did Kant, have seen it as the most interesting and subtle argument for the existence of God. The others are simply nonsense. The ontological argument, beginning with Anselm, Archbishop of Canterbury, purports to establish God's existence from the conception of his perfection. For, if God did not exist, it would be a derogation from His perfection.

Q.: Well, Barth ultimately rejects the ontological argument, too.

J.W.: Does he? He rejects it in the form that Kant disposed of it, when he argued that "existence is not a predicate." That Kantian statement is certainly a valid assertion. The existential import of *something* certainly cannot be treated as an adjective, like "red", or "five fingered", or "good" for something or other. One must treat existences differently. Mathematics points the way here. There are so-called "existence" proofs in mathematics and logic, but the existences they demonstrate are always derived from the unquestioned existence of *something* prior. The philosopher Ajdukiewicz, who founded "radical conventionalism," after a lifetime of dialectic changes, ended up as a "radical empiricist," in that he demanded that existence proofs be given even for tautologies.

Q.: But, how is this applicable to "faith"? Even granting that the Evangelists and the Apostles were "persuading" their hearers of the truth of their message after the fashion of the philosophers.

J.W.: You will note that Christ is represented in this rhetorical scheme of things as the perfect man, particularly in Hebrews. As long as the disciples and their listeners believed that Jesus had been seen alive after he was dead, there was no need for anything beyond the testimony of reputable eye-witnesses, particularly since, among the Gentiles, there was no town in which Paul preached that did not "know" of such resuscitations. But, after the long awaited Messiah did not come, and the conviction of the first generation had died out or down, persuasion must necessarily have taken a different form. Christ is now represented as having been alive (and the evidence for *that* is hardly worse than for the existence of Abraham Lincoln) *and* as the perfection of man and the Law. Here we have the necessary "perfect existence", and *not* as a "predicate." Can we argue from the perfection of Christ, if we can be brought to assent to it, to the essentials of the Christian message? I do not know; but, that, I think, is nevertheless what the Apostles tried to do. And here we find the existence of God given, if it is given at all, in a specifically *Christian* form. Most philosophers, even Bertrand Russell, when they have considered the ontological argument attentively, have experienced that illumination, the persuasion of the truth of this argument, comes fitfully, but with enormous persuasiveness. It comes and goes like those pictures of steps on a paper used by psychologists. First you see them coming out of the paper, then you see them going into the paper, and conversely. When you see them coming out, you cannot imagine how you could ever have seen them going in, even though you have a *recollection* that it *was* so. Some people, as the unknown author of Hebrews urges Christians to do, take the recollection of perfect persuasion *once experienced* as final. Jean Bosc did that in Ellul's account. He did the *tour* of biblical hermeneutics and exegesis and then deemed it of no account to do it further. Ellul makes the point that new questions always arise for *him* that make the *tour* necessary over and over again, particularly as new problems arise. He does this sort of interpretation in an immensely subtle way, with particular attention paid to the various levels of discourse, that is, myth, legend, real history, and so on. What may be the condition of *his* faith, while wrestling with some new problem that the world throws up, I don't know. Perhaps he doesn't either. We, like the electron making quantum jumps, are in a describable state at one time, and in another describable state at another, without even *in principle* knowing or being able to describe what is happening in between.

Q.: Do you think that this account of the Christian message and its "persuasiveness" would be accepted by Ellul? He, like Barth, hasn't much regard for speculative inquiry of a purely philosophic sort, as Heidegger, for example, carries it on.

J.W.: I don't think that Ellul at the present moment would accept my speculations here, even though I could cite numerous passages from his books that tell me at least that that is what he himself is coming to. Of course, for Barth and Ellul, only in God are the contradictions perfectly resolved, e.g., between willing and doing, or between knowledge and action. These are immediate postulates and not reasonings. *That* would please Ellul. For man, there is always a lacuna that expresses itself in our inability to carry out to perfection our arguments. There must therefore be a residual doubt. The meaning of this doubt is simply that we are not gods. That means, too, that the perpetually recurring uncertainty of the ontological argument is structural. Men, who are so confused with respect to the things of *this* world, cannot be expected to reach perfect agreement about things eschatological. And, another thing, the ontological argument is different *from all the others* in that it is immediate. That is to say, no mediating inferences lie between the facts and the "conclusion". It is simply grasped, in the way that Plato's philosopher-king grasped that the formerly hypothetical was unhypothetical. I want to make one thing clear in all this. I don't want these "speculative" theories to be considered as some sort of recondite philosophy. It's well enough to speak of the ontological argument; but the immediacy of it makes it direct experience. Anyhow, we must go as far as reason and intuition allow, and the Christian, who according to Ellul is "standing at the intersection of this world and the next," can and must bear a clear if not an adequate testimony. Perfect agreement is excluded, even between the master and the disciples.

You know, Ellul has become one of those persons about whom people write doctoral dissertations. He will have to get used to students of his thought coming up with suggestions that he might find out of line with what he has written up to a certain point. Sometimes these suggestions will represent improvements, and in that case, ought to be adopted into his own schemata. Sometimes not. It might be well to remember that Leibnitz correctly said that the philosophers tended to be right in what they affirmed and wrong in what they denied.

Q.: You have the last word if you want it. . . .

J.W.: Well, one thing strikes me as particularly significant about Ellul's *Technological Society*. He made his social predictions in 1954, and even earlier. No one listened. His "defeatism", which is certainly not to be found in him or in his book, was violently attacked. That was true even as late as 1964 in the United States. *Now*, the warnings contained in the book are looked upon as dreadful and imminent possibilities by most sensible men. Many think it too late to do anything, except perhaps to pick up the pieces and to go on as well as we can after the crash, when our technological prodigality has at last come home. There is a whole industry of savants recently come into existence, particularly in America, that concern themselves with "futurology." But the warnings these "para-military intellectuals" issue are almost always warnings, not of something in a manageable future, but predictions of the past about which we can almost certainly do nothing. If someone else ever comes

182

along again in the prophetic strain of Ellul, I think it would be useful if he were to be taken seriously while there was yet time. Unfortunately, we don't have any theory of social time, and it *is* admittedly difficult to say what one means by "having time". The long run today looks short enough. I wrote once in connection with Ellul's methodology, that he reduces, for admirably dialectical clarity, everything *ad absurdum*, but that fortunately the world seldom lets things go that far. I was wrong and Ellul was right. The world *does* let its crises go to the absurd, that is, past a point of no return. Ellul has given his witness and it was not heeded. That was right and good for his soul but possibly of little use now to anyone else. We just don't recognize temporal novelty when we confront it. Perhaps this defect is irremediable until the day when we shall all at last be transfigured. If you don't want to wait that long, I suggest, now that everyone is making prophecies about the seventies, that with Ellul and Barth we are entering a decade of a theologically radical interpretation of the social. I hope that the Churches and their house theologians won't stand in the way. If they do, they will be just thrown on the dump heap of history, paradoxically as Christianity makes a comeback.

Q.: I cannot resist one last question: Don't you feel that Christianity occupies in the thought of Barth and Ellul too exclusive a position, at least in the sense that non-Christian religions are neglected?

J.W.: You are certainly right. Anyhow, Mircea Eliade has raised this very objection. Reference to non-Christian religions, except for Judaism, are lacking in these two men. They can and do take seriously the theologies of Marx, Dostoievsky, and so on. But, an *Auseinandersetzung* with Asia is just not there. That represents a whole program for the future.

MA